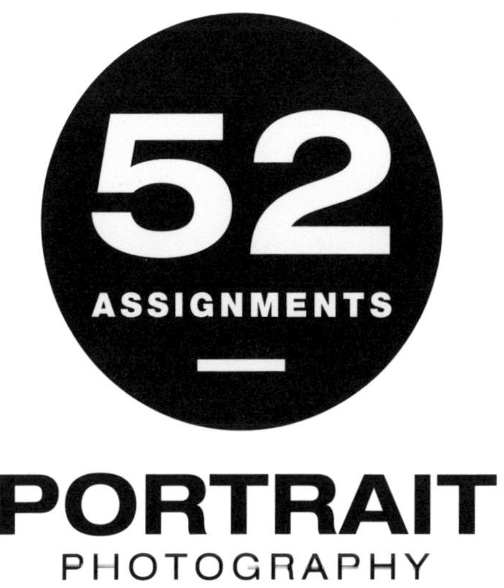

PORTRAIT
PHOTOGRAPHY

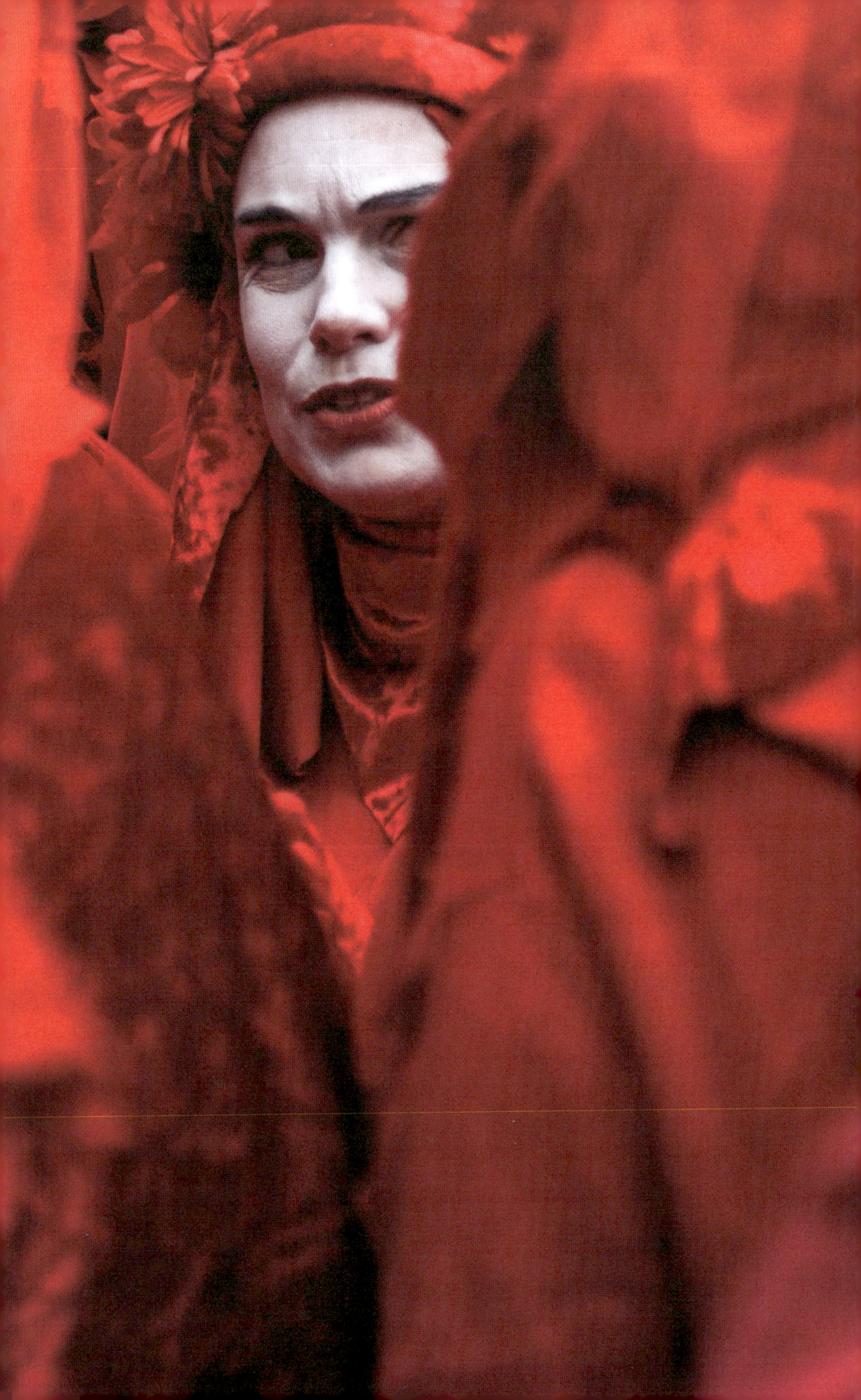

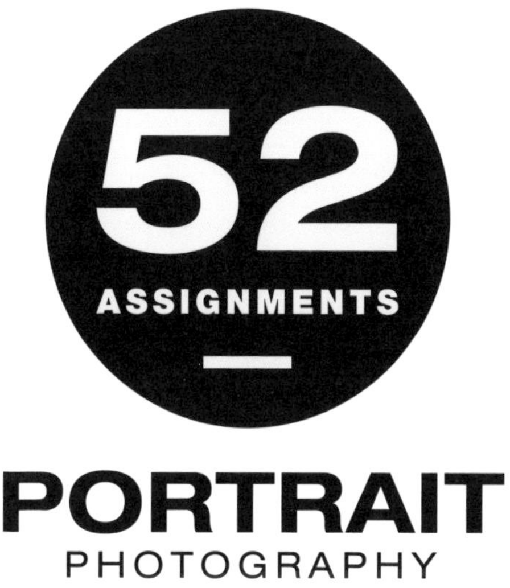

52 ASSIGNMENTS

PORTRAIT
PHOTOGRAPHY

BRIAN LLOYD DUCKETT

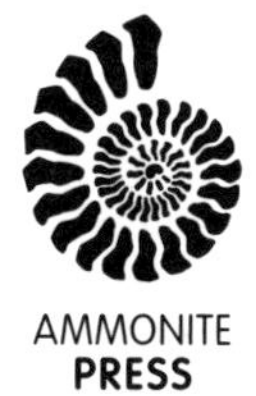

AMMONITE
PRESS

ASSIGNMENTS

Tick off your completed projects

ASSIGNMENT KEY

Each assignment has symbols showing the type of tasks involved.

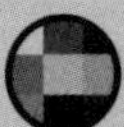 LIGHTING

 CREATIVITY

 TECHNIQUE

 LOCATION

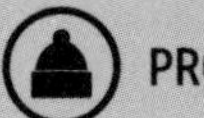 PROPS

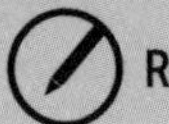 RESEARCH

ASSIGNMENT JOURNAL

Use the journal spaces throughout the book to keep a record of your experimental assignments and images.

INTRODUCTION

In an age when everyone has a camera with them all the time, taking pictures of people has become an integral part of our daily lives. However, there is something special about the art of shooting portraits. It goes beyond simply pointing a lens and clicking a button. It's about more than knowing the techniques or being the master of your camera—it's about being able to engage and connect with your model so that you can squeeze every bit of potential from their time in front of the camera.

Portraits have power. They can reveal the essence of a person, their personality, emotions, state of mind, beauty, frailties, and insecurities. And, of course, their story.

The art of portrait photography started in the mid-19th century with the advent of the daguerreotype, the first commercially successful photographic process. During the late 19th and early 20th centuries, photographers embraced pictorialism, which aimed to elevate photography to the status of fine art. Pictorialist portraits were characterized by soft-focus techniques, artistic manipulation of the negative, and atmospheric elements. You can imagine the dreamlike pictures of early movie stars, politicians, and your distant relatives.

The 20th century brought significant changes to how portraits were shot. The modernist movement brought forth a more direct and documentary style, influenced by advancements in camera technology and social changes.

Pioneers such as Edward Steichen and August Sander aimed to capture the essence of their subjects through straightforward and honest portrayals. In the mid-20th century, fashion and celebrity photography gained prominence, with figures such as Richard Avedon and Irving Penn starting to shape the industry.

Fast-forward to today and we can see that portrait photography has continued to evolve at an even faster pace with the advent of digital cameras and post-production technology. The rise of social media and smartphone photography has made personal expression more accessible to a wider audience, the "selfie" now being part of our everyday existence. As contemporary portrait photographers, we can now experiment with numerous styles, techniques, and approaches, ranging from traditional studio portraits to candid street photography and conceptual art.

Throughout this fascinating history, the portrait has been a powerful way of capturing the human condition and experience, documenting social change, and conveying personal narratives. It remains an enduring and celebrated genre in the world of photography. And portrait photography is something we can all enjoy—it's accessible, challenging, and fun.

Brian Lloyd Duckett

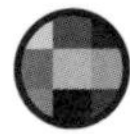

TECHNIQUE

- If you're using natural light, a cloudy but bright day is best, but avoid "panda eyes"—dark eye sockets caused by overhead lighting (it's handy to have a reflector to eliminate this).

- If using artificial light, a two-light setup works well, with both lights set to a similar output (a 4:3 or a 3:2 power ratio should be ideal).

- Aim for a slightly overexposed image to achieve the desired bright and airy look. Use your camera's exposure compensation or manual mode to increase the exposure or adjust the settings in post-production if shooting in Raw.

- Choose a plain light background without artefacts or detail—too much clutter will result in a messy portrait.

- Bounce light back onto any shady areas using a reflector (or large sheet of white card).

- A little overexposure will help emphasize the high-key effect.

ASSIGNMENT JOURNAL

____

____

____

____

____

____

PRO TIP

If you're using a light modifier such as a softbox or umbrella for even and flattering lighting, the bigger the better. The larger the light source, the softer the light and the more gradual the tonal transitions.

THE BRIGHT ONES

The high-key portrait is characterized by a bright and evenly lit subject and a predominantly bright background. The lighting is generally set up to minimize shadows and create a soft, bright, and ethereal look.

It's all about subtlety, creating a flattering and youthful appearance for your subject. The even lighting helps to smooth out imperfections in the skin and the bright background helps to create a sense of calmness.

Your aim for this assignment is to create a portrait using bright lighting to eliminate shadow areas, producing an even, serene, and ethereal effect. This can be achieved with one light and a reflector or, more simply, by using soft natural light from a window or outdoors. A lens with a focal length of 85mm or slightly longer is ideal for a high-key portrait, especially when used with a wide aperture of f/1.4 or f/1.8, which will allow for a gradual fall-off in focus beyond the eyes, adding to the ethereal look.

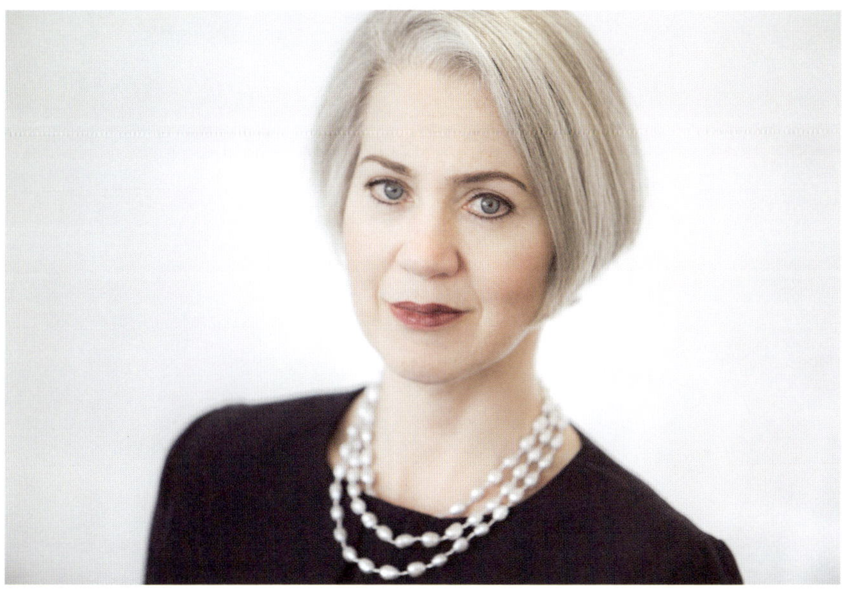

▲ *You'll often see high-key portraits in black and white; where color is used, the colors are very subtle and sometimes used as an accent (in this case, the red lips).*

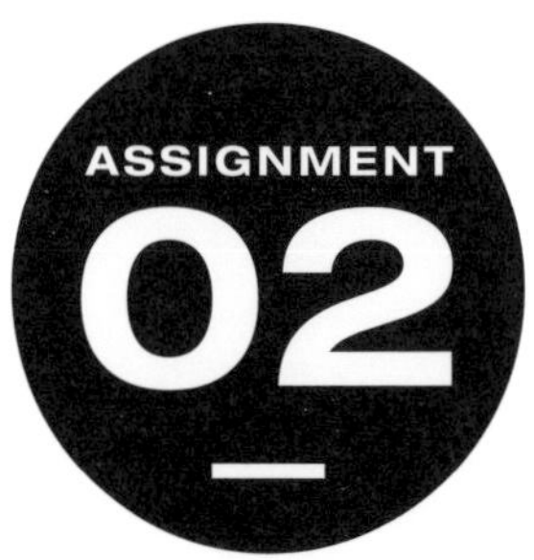

ASSIGNMENT

02

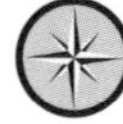

ASSIGNMENT JOURNAL

____

____

____

____

____

____

____

____

____

____

TECHNIQUE

- When you arrive at the location, take time to study the backgrounds and the light to help you understand where your best compositions will be.

- Try different lighting setups before you shoot: will you use flash, natural light, or a combination? Use ambient light if you can—this will help you create a more compelling and believable image.

- Study all the elements in the background: what will support your subject's story and what will detract from it?

- Beware of clutter and remove anything that will be in the way—a large part of any location photography is furniture removal!

- Shoot handheld if you can—you'll have more freedom and fluidity than you would have using a tripod.

- Use a reflector to bounce light into any areas of unwanted shadow.

PRO TIP

Take a selection of lenses with a variety of focal lengths (bear in mind you'll probably be shooting wide for most shots). A focal length of between 28mm and 50mm should work fine for an environmental portrait, the ideal being around 35mm; this allows you to get close enough to the person while capturing plenty of interesting background information.

ENVIRONMENTAL PORTRAIT

This type of portrait is all about the connection between an individual and their environment, whether this is somewhere they work, live, or play. The background is just as important as the subject and often helps build a strong narrative.

For this assignment, you're going to shoot an environmental portrait that says something about your subject's profession, hobby, or interest. Your subject could be a friend in their home, a work colleague, a local business, or an artist—anyone who inhabits an interesting environment.

Get to know your subject and develop a relationship in advance of the shoot. Check out their website. If they have performed any interviews, look them up. Even better, chat to them in person or over the phone, and try to visit the location and get a feel for it—and work out your creative approach and pre-visualize the image.

▼ *It's essential to balance the light in the background with the light on the subject—they're just as important as each other.*

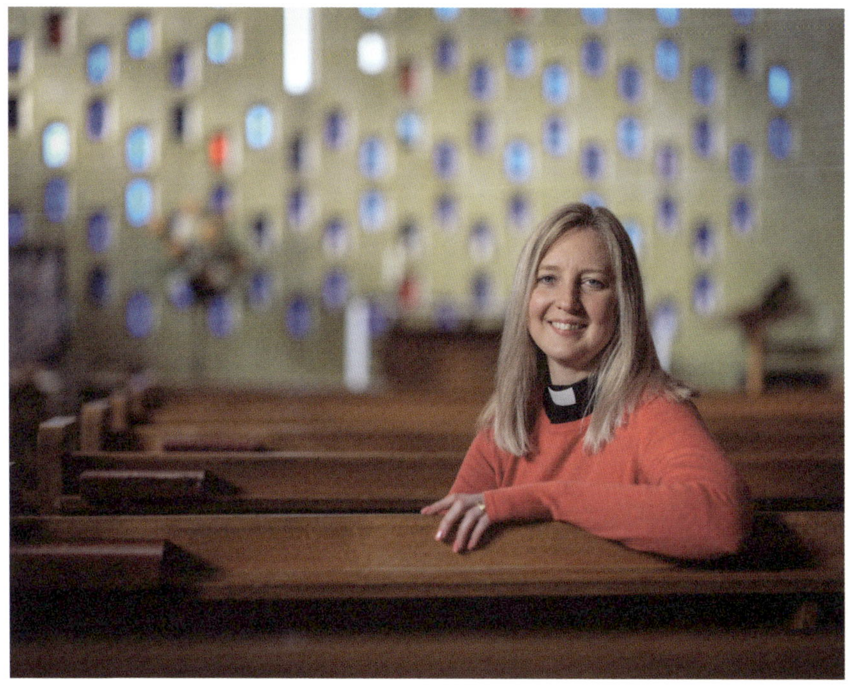

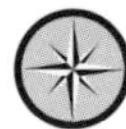

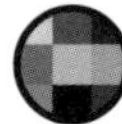

TECHNIQUE

- Leave the flash at home and use natural lighting, whether the portrait is indoors or out. Shooting in the shade often works well and is more flattering than in direct light.

- Outdoor lighting can be unpredictable, and a large white reflector can be useful for bouncing light back onto faces, particularly to avoid "panda eyes."

- Encourage the family to interact with each other, chatting, laughing, and behaving as they would if you weren't there rather than posing stiffly for the camera.

- Have plenty of jokes and funny stories ready for when you need some spontaneous interactions.

- Don't forget you can include yourself if you're shooting your own family—just pop your camera on a tripod and set the self-timer.

CAPTURE A FAMILY MOMENT

Gone are the days when families posed stiffly in the studio for their annual portrait, awaiting the instruction "Say cheese!" from the photographer. Things have moved on and family portraits now tend to be much more relaxed and focused on fun rather than rigidly documenting a stage in people's lives.

Your brief is to shoot an informal portrait of a family having fun, interacting with each other in attractive surroundings. Choose a comfortable location, ideally an outdoor one which your subjects are familiar with and will feel relaxed in, such as a garden, park, or beach. Suggest your subjects dress down and wear whatever they would normally wear, rather than dressing up for the occasion, and encourage the younger ones to bring along their favorite toys to keep them occupied. If there's a family pet, include it in the shoot—it's probably as much a part of the family as the children are.

For a relaxed and natural family portrait such as this, you should aim to shoot outdoors in bright but overcast light either early or late in the day, avoiding contrasty sunlight and overly harsh shadows.

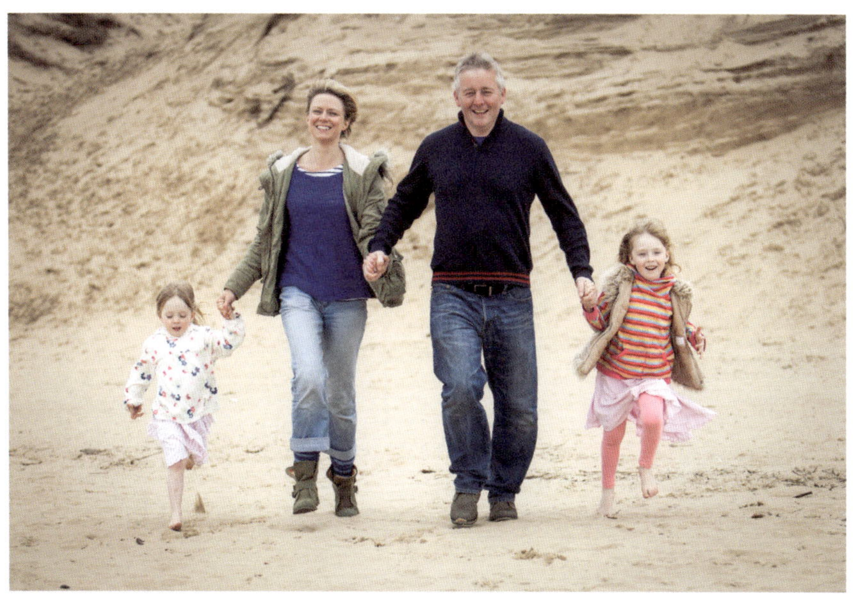

▲ *Lots of movement and energy are great for this style of portrait, with nothing too staged or posed.*

ASSIGNMENT JOURNAL

____

____

____

____

____

____

____

PRO TIP

Avoid the mistake of using too wide an aperture if people are on different planes throughout the frame—f/8 or f/11 should ensure that everyone is in focus—and remember to use a fast shutter speed (at least 1/1250 sec.) if the family is engaged in some activity. It's also a good idea to set your camera to continuous/burst mode to make sure you capture all the interesting "micro moments."

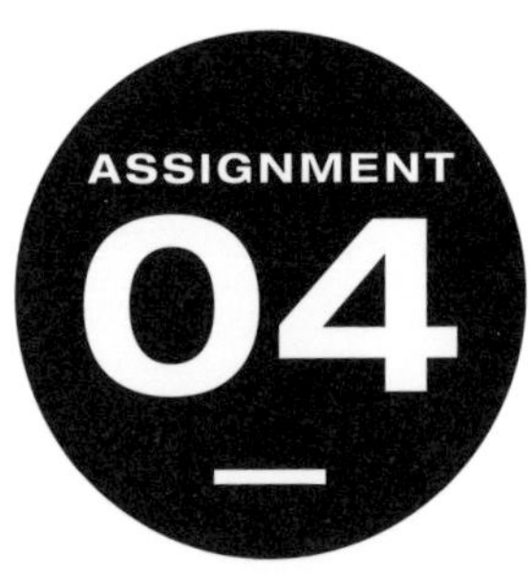

ASSIGNMENT 04

TECHNIQUE

- Play with different light sources, such as natural light, artificial light, or a combination of both. You could also try colored gels or create interesting shadows to add texture and depth to your portrait.

- Experiment with whacky perspectives, angles, and framing to create an unexpected and striking composition; consider using negative space, patterns, or leading lines.

- Think about bright or contrasting colors— or maybe shoot in black and white.

ASSIGNMENT JOURNAL

PRO TIP

Don't be constrained by "what's been done before"—this is where you can get really creative and produce something unique. You may find an effect or technique you really like and then go on to produce a set of portraits on the same theme using different subjects.

▶ *This full-length portrait, which was used in a business context, was created using a slow shutter speed to give a sense of movement and energy.*

GET ABSTRACT

Portraits are usually taken to reveal the subject's character, looks, or personality, or to tell a particular story. However, rather than focusing solely on the physical attributes of the subject, abstract portrait photography may emphasize elements such as color, shape, or composition to create a visually compelling image.

In this assignment, you'll abandon convention and shoot an abstract portrait. Don't be afraid to experiment and be creative—as with other forms of abstract photography, anything goes. Here are a few ideas to get you started:

- Shoot through a layer such as a misted-up window, a veil, or shattered glass.
- Experiment with extremes of light and shade.
- Use colored light bulbs (or place colored gels over your light source) to bathe your subject's face in strange light.
- Create multiple exposures.
- Use intentional camera movement (ICM) to bring a dynamic look to the portrait.
- Shoot with a fisheye lens to radically distort the perspective.
- Introduce the abstraction in post-production—for example, make a pop-art image or a duotone.

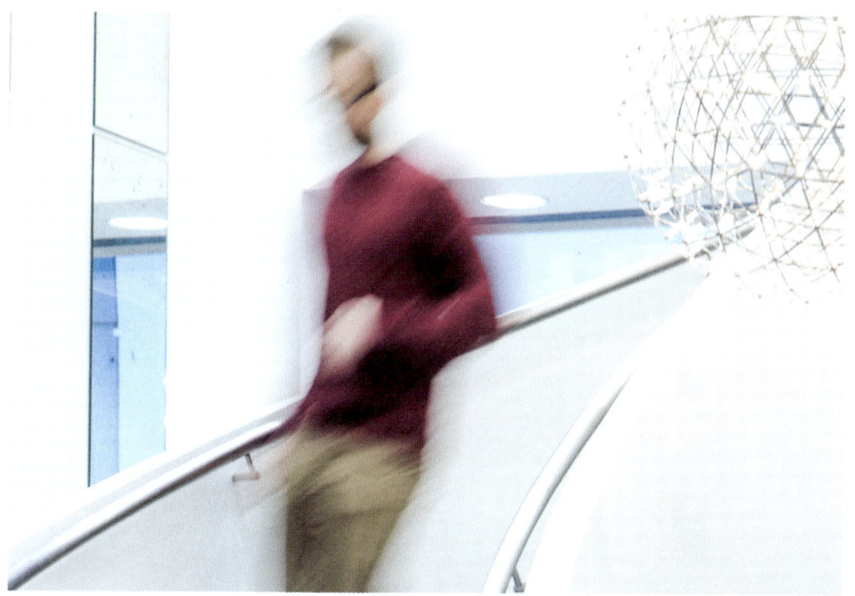

TECHNIQUE

- Aim for a bright, almost high-key result (see Assignment #1) and don't worry too much if some of the highlights seem too bright—this can enhance the overall effect.

- You may find it easier to focus manually rather than to rely on autofocus, which often "hunts" and struggles to decide what you want to focus on.

- Look closely at what is in the reflected background—does it add to or detract from the portrait? A wide aperture (generally, the wider the better) will help blur out any distracting background information.

REFLECTED GLORY

We're going to shoot through a window, making the reflections on the glass a key part of the image—a deliberate design feature rather than something you would normally try to eliminate. When used in this way, reflections can bring something extra to the party—a sense of intimacy, dreaminess, or even voyeurism. Try this anywhere—at home, in café windows, through the car window, either with someone who is posing for you or even as a candid portrait of a stranger. It's an easy technique to master and the results can be stunning.

Move around and adjust your shooting position so that the reflections are in the right place in the frame and watch how the light changes as the camera angle moves. Make sure that nothing too distracting or irrelevant is caught in the reflection (such as you, your camera bag, or a white van), and shoot with the widest aperture possible to add depth and isolate the subject's face. Use manual focusing, as autofocus will usually struggle to work out where you want the point of focus to be.

PRO TIP

When you first look at the images on your computer, they may look a little flat and one-dimensional. You'll probably find that an increase in contrast and/or clarity, bringing out the overall contrast and the midtone contrast, will enhance them significantly.

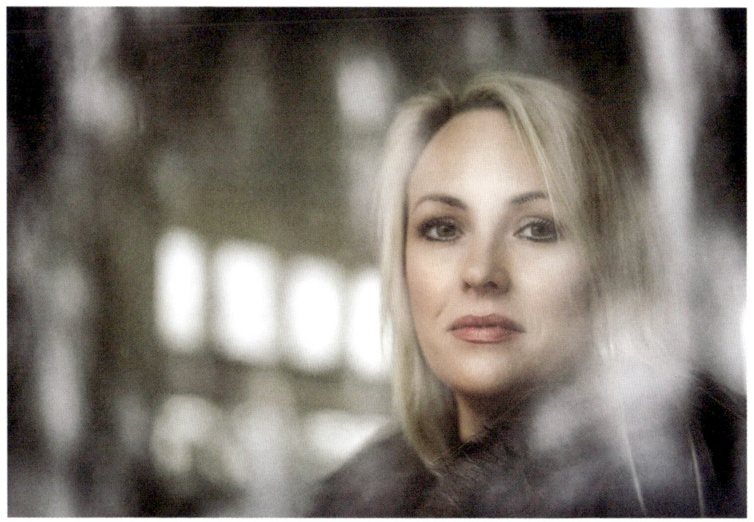

▲ *These shots work well when your model has a pensive expression, with the reflections providing a dreamy layer over the face.*

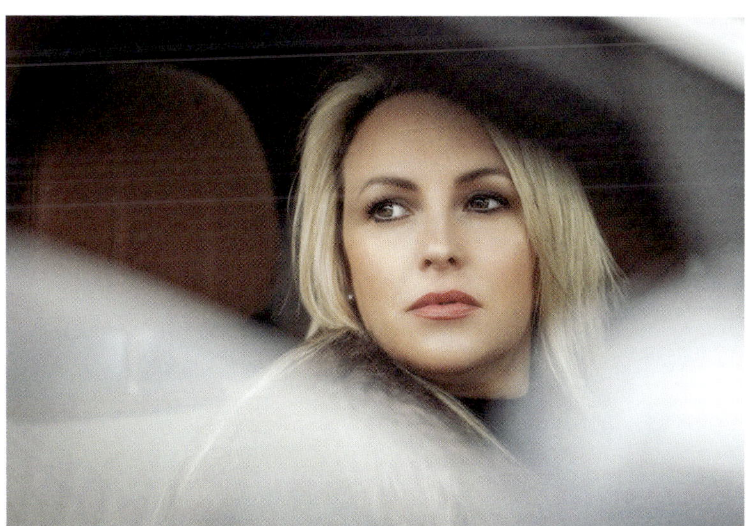

▲ *Same model, different look. Here the face is fully visible, but we use the reflections on the car window as a design feature.*

TECHNIQUE

- Position the light carefully. Experiment with different angles and distances to find the right position for your subject and the type of image you want to create.

- Bear in mind that with any light source, the closer it is to the subject, the softer it will be so don't be afraid to position the light as close as you can.

- Try different power settings, adjusting the exposure accordingly, and see how the effect varies. Start with a low power setting (1/4 power) and work up from there.

JUST ONE LIGHT

Who needs lots of lighting gear to create striking studio portraits? This assignment is proof that you don't, as you'll be shooting a portrait using just one light.

Don't see the one-light approach as a limiting factor—think of it as a creative choice. For this assignment, you won't need a studio, just one lighting source, which could be a flash head, studio head, or continuous light. This is all about experimentation— using your single light, try lots of different positions and power settings and you'll see how many effects can be achieved, from a lovely "plain vanilla" portrait to something more creative.

Pay attention to shadows. With only one light source, shadows can be more pronounced, so consider their direction and intensity in your composition.
You can use a reflector to fill in shadows or position the light to intensify them.

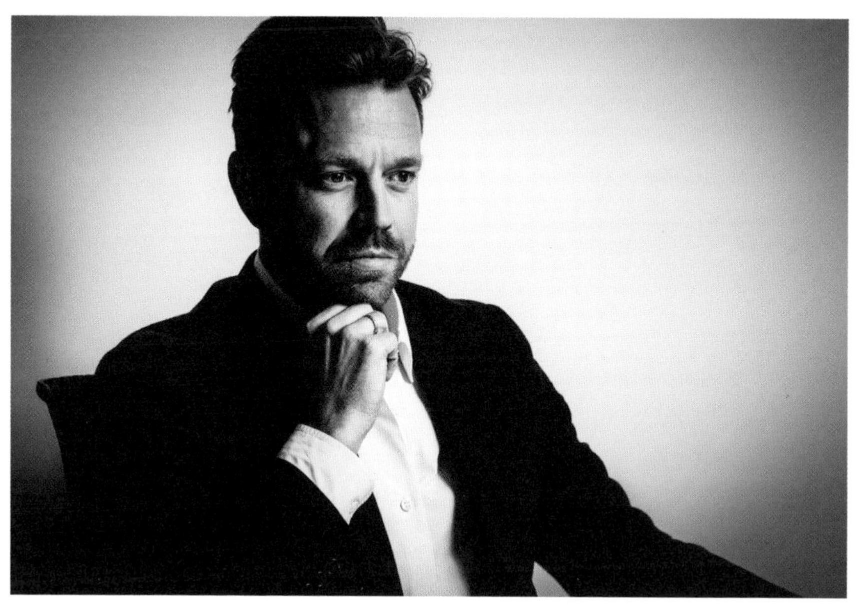

▲ *You'll have more creative options than you think with just one light, from a relatively contrasty look like this, with the light positioned to one side of the subject, to something much softer, with the light closer to the camera's axis.*

ASSIGNMENT JOURNAL

PRO TIP

Use light modifiers such as umbrellas, softboxes, and reflectors to shape the light to achieve different effects. Umbrellas are a cheap and easy-to-use option—the bigger the umbrella, the softer the light. A softbox will give a flattering, diffused effect and should be used as close to the subject as possible for maximum softness. A reflector can be seen as extra light in itself, illuminating darker areas of the face.

TECHNIQUE

- Spend time talking to your subject before the shoot and try to understand what makes them tick and what drives their passion.

- Make the point of the picture obvious—it will lose impact if viewers are expected to do too much guessing about what it's all about.

- Aim for simple, bold shapes and strong colors.

- Avoid high contrast and keep the lighting flat and even so that it doesn't distract; if you're shooting outdoors, shoot on a bright but overcast day or in a well-shaded area.

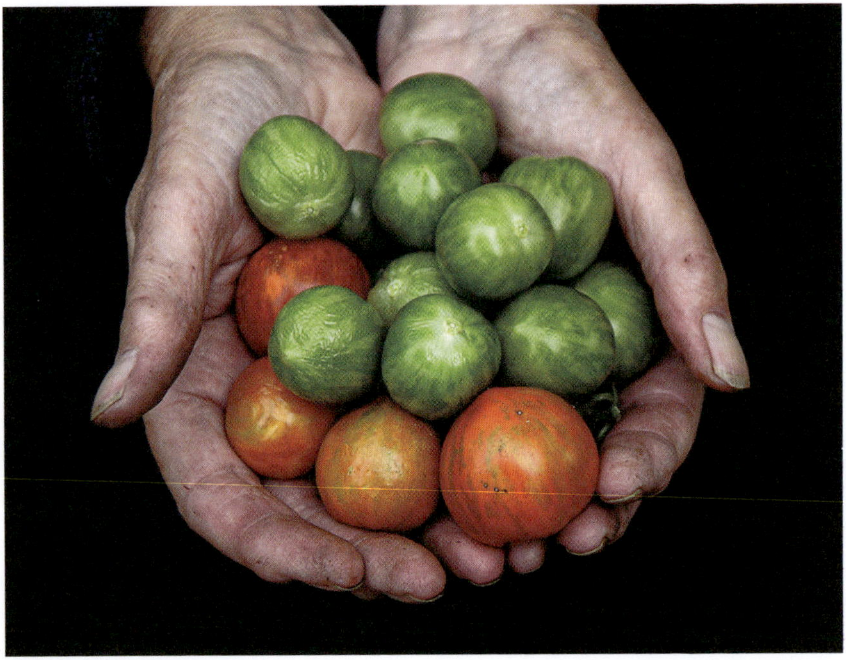

GIVE US A CLUE

There's more to photographing people than their faces. This exercise is designed to help you really think hard about your subject. What things really feature in their lives? What's important to them? How can you tell their story without revealing their face?

The example used here is a photograph of a gardener who spends her life growing plants, flowers, fruit, and vegetables. The picture of just her hands, ingrained with soil and showing the signs of many cold years spent outdoors, reveals much more about her than a picture of her face might.

A minimalist approach usually works well. Avoid background clutter and get straight to the detail—the picture will lose its focus and sense of purpose if there are other distracting elements in the frame. Do your research and try to find an angle for your shot (don't go in cold, hoping to find something as you go along).

PRO TIP

Try shooting with a longer focal length—between 85mm to 135mm—to compress the perspective and to isolate the crucial detail. Use as wide an aperture as you can, finding just the right balance between blurring the background and keeping all the areas of the "feature" (such as the hands) sharp.

ASSIGNMENT JOURNAL

◀ *A simple image with strong shapes and bold colors will focus the viewer's attention on what's important.*

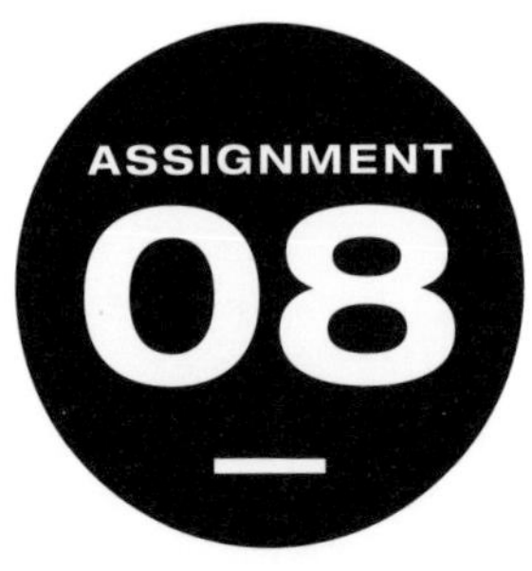

TECHNIQUE

- Use a tripod and maybe ask a friend to pose "in position" for you to help get a perfect composition.

- As with any portrait, the right lighting is critical so find an approach that is flattering, and which conveys the right mood.

- Find a camera angle which suits your face shape, the pose, and the lighting.

- Shoot lots and give yourself as many options as possible, with plenty of variations of pose, lighting mood, and concept.

- If you're using a smartphone, make sure you look into the camera lens rather than the middle of the screen.

THE SELFIE

The self-portrait—"selfie"—has had enduring appeal for decades and we should all take them for a number of reasons: the selfie can help you understand what it's like to be on the other side of the lens, you can practice different posing and lighting techniques, and, like the examples here, it can be a great way to express yourself.

You can take your selfie as a creative experiment, to test a lighting technique, to use on your website or social media profiles—or just for a bit of fun. But don't just plonk yourself in front of your smartphone and press the button—put some thought into it, particularly if you're using a selfie to promote yourself, as you may be judged on it. Be expressive and let your personality come through—don't just gawp at the camera! Don't be afraid to go conceptual (as Neil did, opposite) and try something off the wall. Let your creative juices flow!

The pictures here were shot by street photographer Neil Johansson as part of a "365" project. He shot a selfie every day for a year—now there's commitment for you!

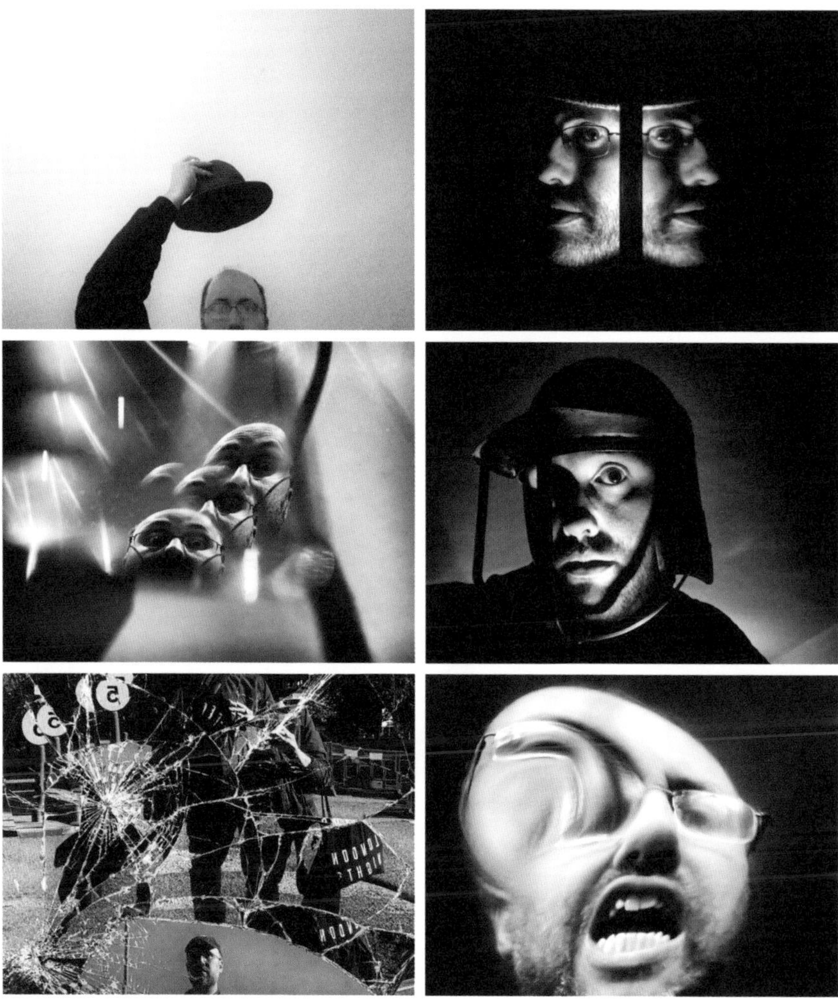

PRO TIP

A little sympathetic post-production will help show you at your best but keep it real and don't overdo it. See this exercise as producing a "serious" selfie and leave out the whacky effects or extensive beautification.

▲ *Neil Johansson (@sven804) took a highly creative approach to selfies and undertook a project which became his daily photographic diary.*

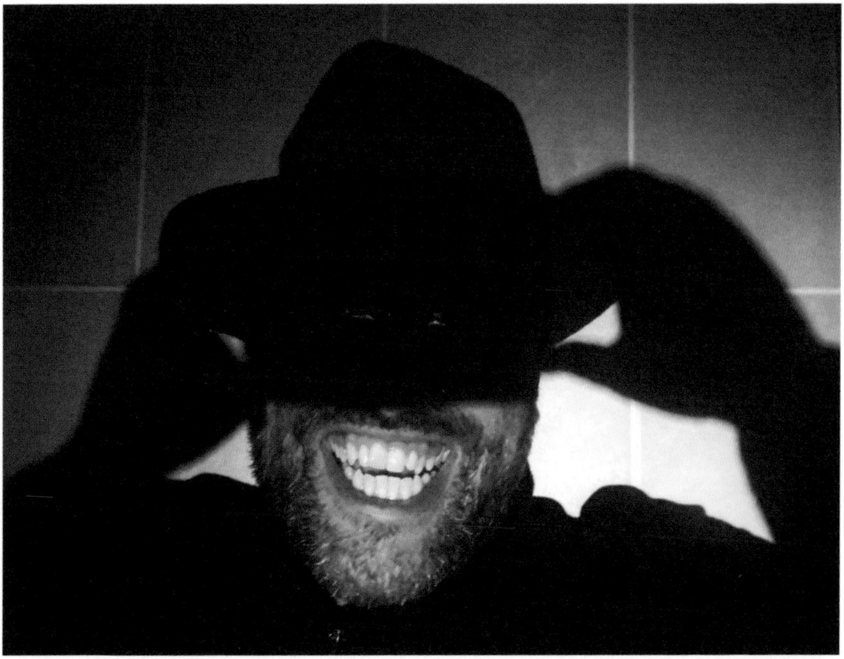

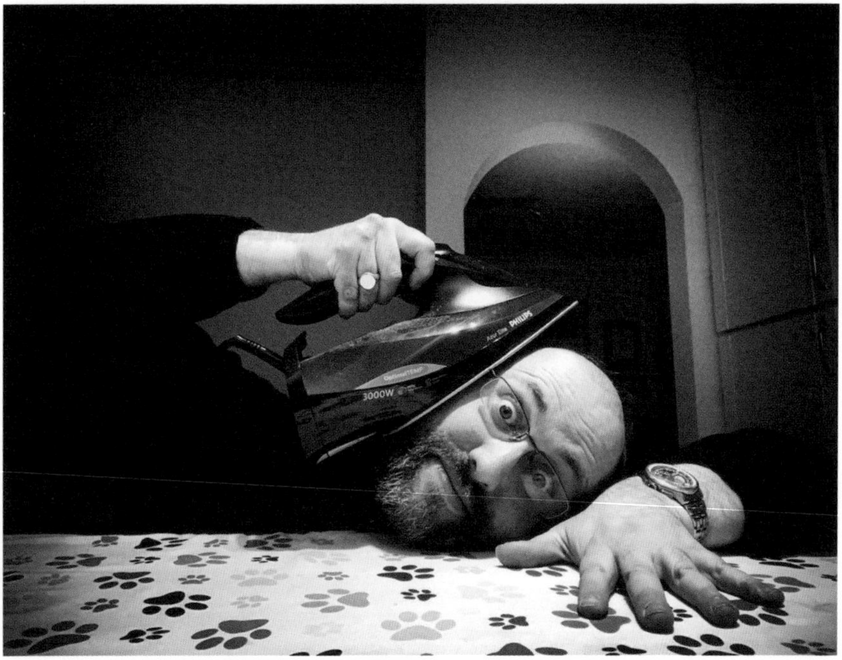

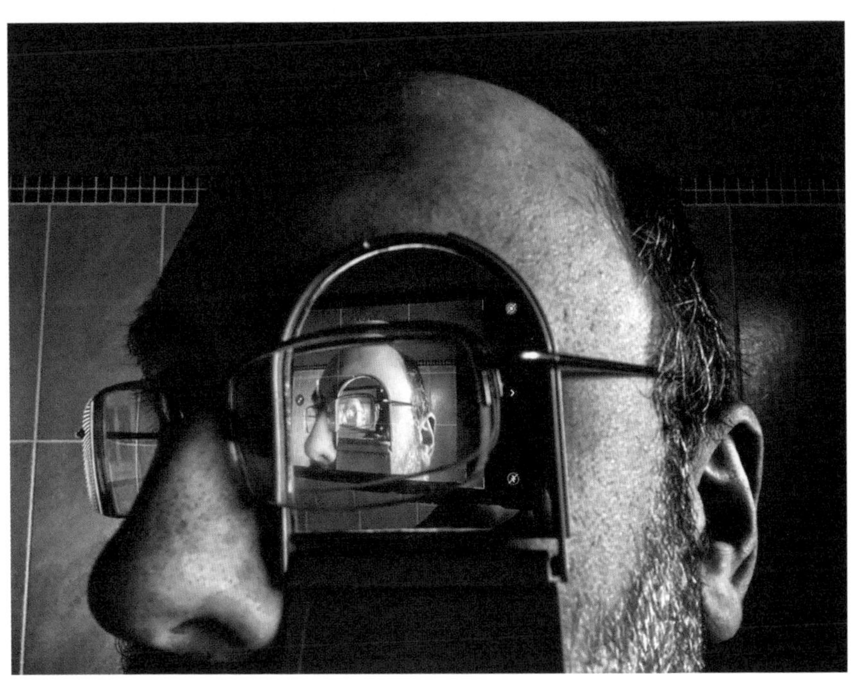

ASSIGNMENT JOURNAL

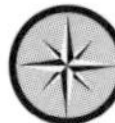

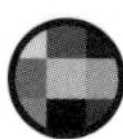

TECHNIQUE

- Decide whether you want the background in or out of focus. Does it add anything to the picture? If not, use a wide aperture such as f/2.8 for a shallow depth of field.

- Remember that you're in charge, so don't be afraid to direct your subject: "Look over there" . . . "Move your arm down a bit" . . . "Let's have a big smile for this one," and so on. People often feel awkward and will welcome the direction.

- Always offer to show your subjects their image on the back of the camera—they'll usually be surprised at how good they look!

STREET LIFE

This exercise is all about street portraits. Street photography generally means candid photography, but this relates to a posed portrait, taken with the knowledge and consent of the subject. You'll almost certainly find that, with a warm and confident approach, nine out of ten people will agree to having their portrait taken. Street portraits are great fun and when you've got a few of these under your belt, you'll probably find the whole thing quite addictive.

Choosing the right subject is the key to success. Go for people who seem to want attention—people who look good, eccentric, outrageous, etc. A little flattery goes a long way—compliment someone's hat, tattoos, or coat and you've already won them over. Say something like "Is it okay if I take your portrait?" and take a moment to move your subject into the best available light and against the best background.

Don't rush it. Once someone has said yes, you have their attention for at least several minutes so make the most of the opportunity. Try several different poses and take as many pictures as you feel you can.

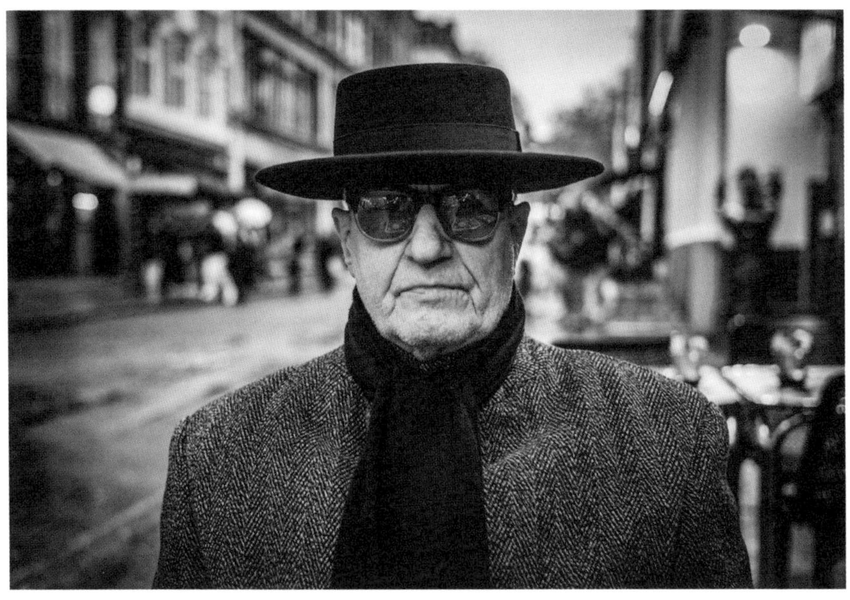

▲ *If you choose someone who looks good,*
they'll nearly always say yes.

ASSIGNMENT JOURNAL

PRO TIP

Strangers tend to be more receptive to having their photo taken if they feel they can trust you're a credible photographer. One way to help with this is to have some business cards printed. If you can show subjects examples of your work, so much the better. This could be on social media, in your smartphone's photos app, or even printed copies. Again, this reinforces your credibility. Always offer to send your subject a copy of the image and take rejection on the chin—it happens! Just move on to the next one.

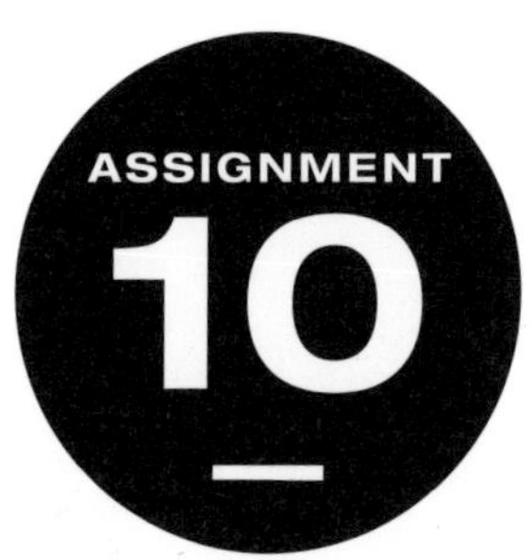

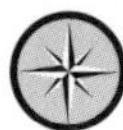

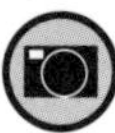

TECHNIQUE

- Animals can move quickly so shoot in burst mode to ensure you capture just the right moment.

- If the pet (and owner) is on the ground, getting down to their eye level will help create a greater sense of intimacy.

- Bring a favorite toy along—this can help keep the animal under control.

- The aim is to capture the bond between pet and owner so look for natural interactions and strong eye contact.

- Animals can be unpredictable so be prepared to wait for the perfect moment.

- Have some treats handy to reward the animal for good behavior.

PET PORTRAIT

Shooting a portrait of a pet with their doting owner can be rewarding and great fun. It can also be challenging because animals are unpredictable, and they can move quickly. Quick reflexes and good communication skills are essential.

This assignment is all about relationships—capturing the bond shared by pet and owner and showing the unique connection between them. You could go for a calm, reflective portrait or a crazy action shot; indoors or outdoors; with one animal or several of them—there are lots of possibilities.

To help the animal feel at ease and behave naturally, choose a location which is familiar and comfortable for them. Use natural light whenever possible, as flash could startle the pet, and because animals tend to move, use as fast a shutter speed as you can—ideally 1/250 sec. or faster (you may need to bump up the ISO to achieve this).

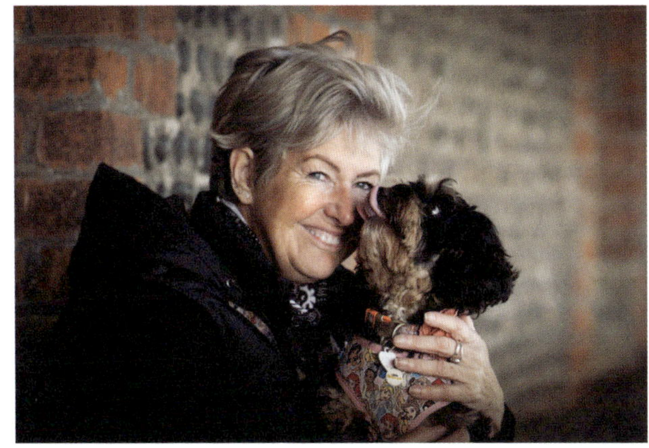

◀ Try to capture a strong bond between the owner and their pet—and don't be afraid to introduce a comical twist.

PRO TIP

Try to spend a little time with the owner and pet so they both (especially the pet) "accept" you and are comfortable in your presence. This should result in more natural behavior and a stronger connection between you and your subjects.

▼ Natural light equals a natural portrait. Here we shot into the sun and used a white reflector to bounce light onto the subjects.

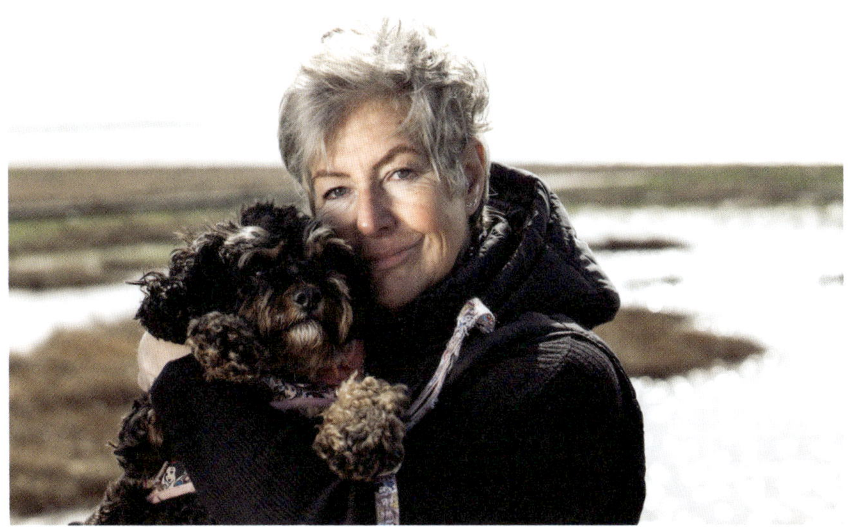

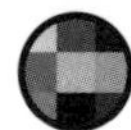
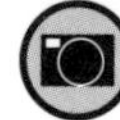

TECHNIQUE

- Keep everything as simple as possible, particularly the lighting. Lots of powerful studio lights can be intimidating and even scary for little ones.

- Use as fast a shutter speed as you can manage (1/1250 sec. or faster)—children often move rather quickly. To achieve this, use a wide aperture and/or higher ISO (around f/2 and ISO 400–800 respectively).

- Natural light is flattering, and children are often more relaxed in an outdoor setting.

- Children often wear bright clothes so be aware of any color clashes with the background.

THE YOUNG ONES

Remember the advice actors were always given: never work with children or animals? It doesn't apply to portrait photographers. With their ease in front of the camera, their smiles, and their natural expressions, children make great subjects for portraits.

This assignment is an exercise in photographing a child—anyone from a baby to a teenager. You can do this indoors or outside, using natural or artificial light (natural light is often best when working with little ones, as big bright lights can be intimidating). A focal length between 50mm and 85mm will allow you to keep enough distance to help the child to behave naturally. Try to do this early in the day when the light is soft, and the young ones still have lots of energy and attention span.

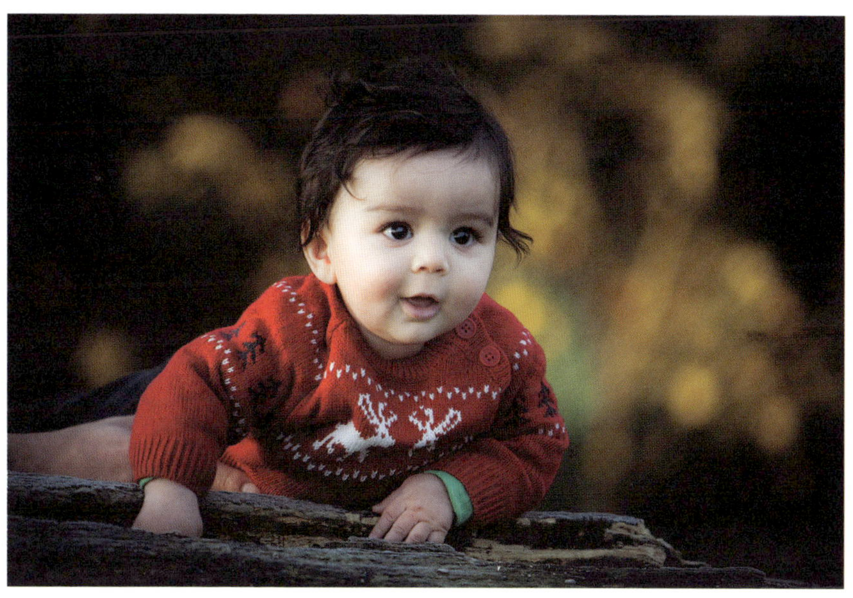

▲ *Outdoor locations are ideal, with soft natural light and a more relaxed atmosphere than in the studio.*

ASSIGNMENT JOURNAL

PRO TIP

The more you can prepare beforehand, especially if using studio lights, the less time children will have to get bored or distracted. Bring some props along—balls, favorite toys, pets, etc.—and give your subject something to do. Let younger children be themselves and snap away while they're engaged in something they enjoy—telling them to look at the camera or smile can make them freeze and you won't get a spontaneous, natural portrait.

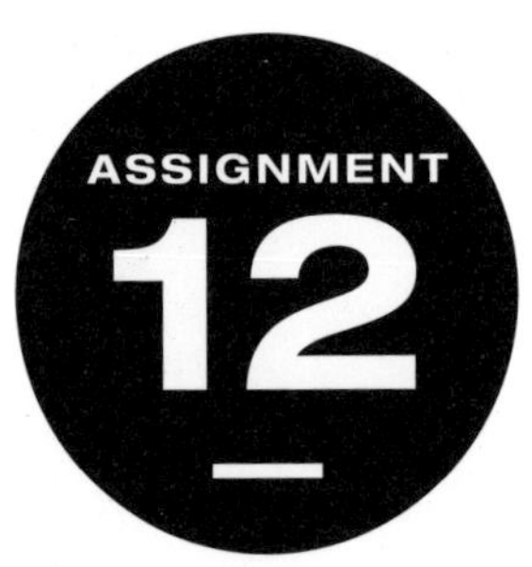

ASSIGNMENT

12

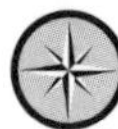

TECHNIQUE

- Find a good source of natural light—this could be outdoors or indoors using the soft diffused light from a window or skylight (though not direct sunlight).

- Pay attention to the details and think about the important objects and accessories that make up the subject's lifestyle, such as books, clothes, or even their favorite cushion.

- Err on the side of overexposure for a laid-back and upbeat vibe.

- Encourage natural and spontaneous interactions between your subjects and capture people engaging in activities they enjoy, including conversations. Encourage them to be themselves and forget that you're there.

PRO TIP

Use "light touch" post-production edits to maintain a realistic and authentic look. Avoid areas of harsh shadow and blown-out highlights and move the Vibrance slider to the left to mute the colors a little for a more natural effect.

▶ *Try to get under the skin of your subject's lifestyle. In this case, their passion for the countryside shines through.*

THE HIGH LIFE

The antithesis of stiff portraits in a studio setting, a lifestyle portrait should aim to capture individuals or groups candidly and naturally, reflecting their everyday lives, activities, and personal style. Unlike traditional portrait photography, lifestyle portraits seek to convey a sense of authenticity, spontaneity, and genuine interaction. The subjects are often photographed in familiar settings such as their homes, workplaces, or favorite outdoor locations rather than in a studio.

For this assignment, you'll shoot a person or a small group in a natural, unposed setting, reflecting their everyday life or a specific activity they're engaged in. The ideal location would be a relaxed setting such as the subject's home, the park, the beach, or a favorite beauty spot.

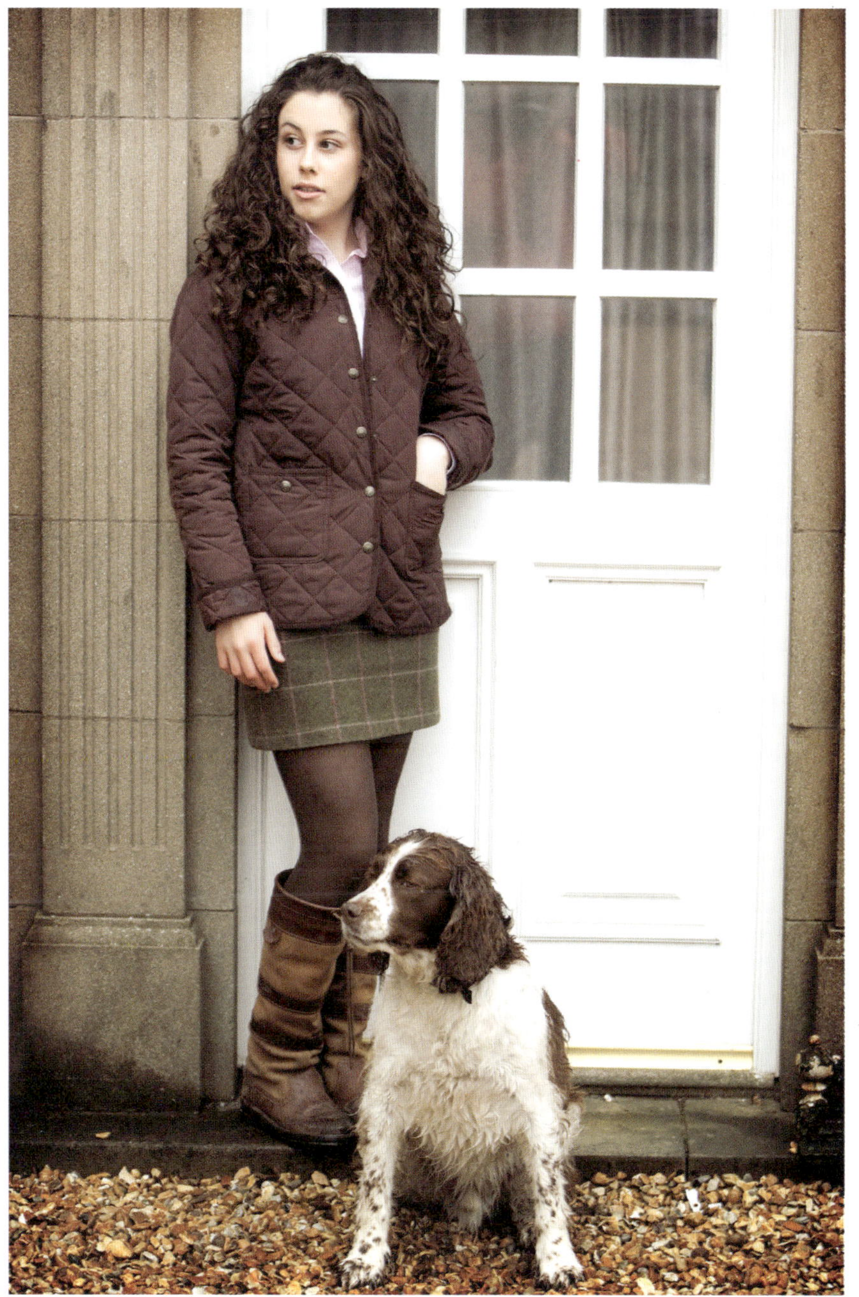

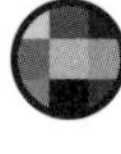

TECHNIQUE

- For a natural and relaxed look, use available rather than artificial light sources wherever possible.

- A focal length of around 85mm will give a natural and flattering perspective and a wide aperture such as f/2 will blur any distracting background while retaining sharpness in the facial features.

- Make lots of small talk—engaging your subject in light conversation will help them to relax.

- Think about and plan your concept long before the shoot and try to match the images with the personality of the business.

- Don't be afraid to direct your subjects— they're probably not used to being photographed in this way.

YOU'RE THE BUSINESS

Business portraits have changed dramatically over the years and the shot of the awkward, stiffly posed executive against the white background is now considered to be a little passé. What we now see much more of is the relaxed, contemporary version which shows more personality and warmth.

Wherever you live, you won't be far from a business, whether it's a huge company or a small entrepreneurial start-up, and it's always worth knocking on a few doors— most businesses would welcome some (free) images for their own marketing or even just their social media profiles.

For this assignment, you'll need to find a business, maybe one owned by a friend or relative, and then ask if you can shoot some portraits. It's worth making it clear that you're doing this to boost your portfolio or develop your skills, and you're not charging for it (more doors will open to you this way). You never know, if they like the pictures they might ask you to come back for a paid gig.

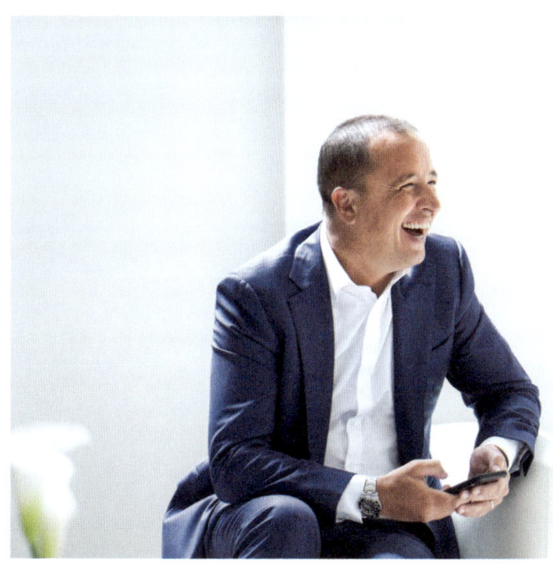

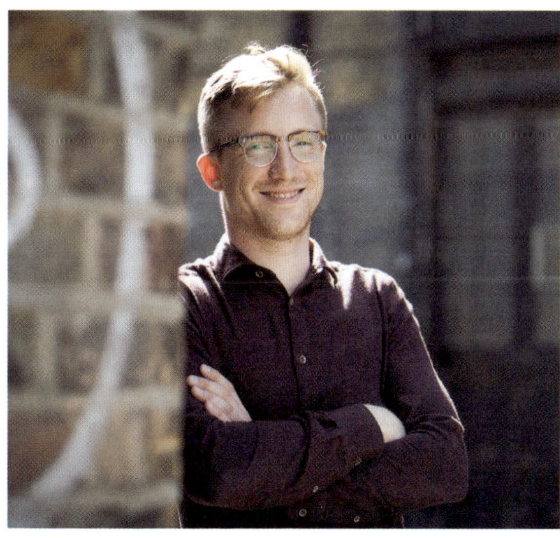

▲ *If you snap your subject when they're in friendly conversation, you should get some lovely, relaxed shots.*

◄ *Shooting toward the sun, with some fill light from a reflector, helps give a bright and modern look.*

PRO TIP

Planning is everything. Look through some magazines and business websites to find some styles you like and then create a mood board to help you get a feel for what you want to achieve (you could use Pinterest for this).

TECHNIQUE

- Aim for a good figure-to-ground ratio—the distance between subject and background—to avoid any unwanted distractions in the frame. The simplest way to achieve this is by using a wide aperture such as f/2.8.

- Use natural light to avoid any flare or hotspots from flash or other artificial light sources.

- Watch out for reflections in windows and on shiny chrome or paintwork.

- Try to include some of the vehicle's detail and character—headlights, grills, and wheels are particular favorites. Add dynamism by using leading lines or by shooting from a very low perspective.

- If you have access to some water (maybe a hosepipe or watering can), the effects of moisture on a vehicle can have a dramatic effect.

ASSIGNMENT JOURNAL

PRO TIP

If you can't find anyone to shoot, visit a classic car or bike show and you'll find no shortage of willing volunteers. Most such shows allow amateur photographers to operate freely, and you wouldn't normally need permission to shoot.

PRIDE AND JOY

Cars, boats, bicycles, scooters . . . it's easy to fall in love with our treasured
mode of transport, our pride and joy. Some of us like getting our hands dirty with
maintenance, others like to polish, nurture, or restore—it's a form of escapism that
provides endless enjoyment to those with a cherished item.

In this assignment, you'll be shooting someone who's passionate about their vehicle,
in this case a car owner. With their chrome, curves, retro color palettes, and nostalgic
design flourishes, classic cars can themselves be objects of beauty. Put all that
together with the proud owner and you have all the ingredients for a great portrait.

All you need to do is find someone who's passionate about their pride and joy
and ask if you can take some portraits of them with their vehicle. Most people will
be flattered and will agree to posing for you in return for a few pictures. Your portrait
could be full length, showing subject and vehicle together as a wide shot, or a close-
up head-and-shoulders shot, perhaps incorporating some interesting detail such as
a chrome wing mirror.

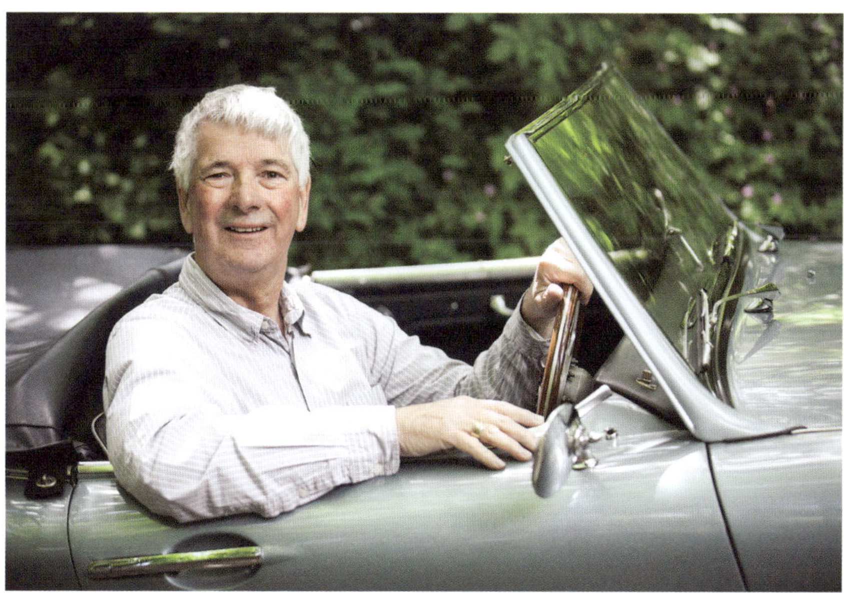

▲ *Shoot a variety of poses, angles, and
ideas. Make the most of your opportunity!*

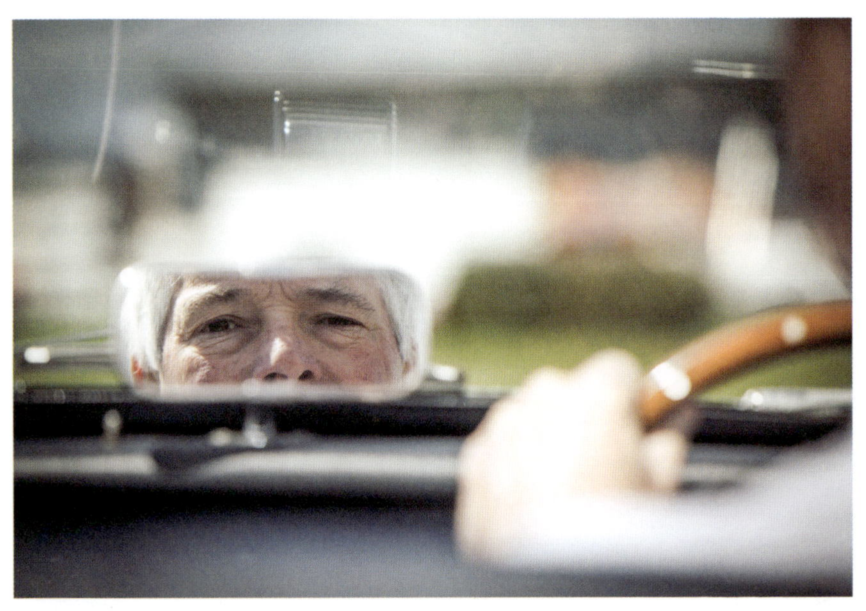

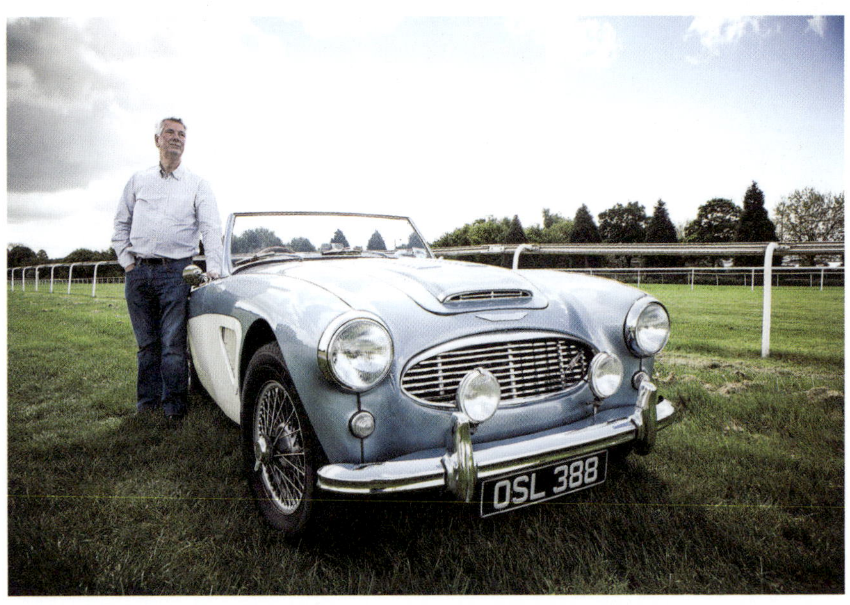

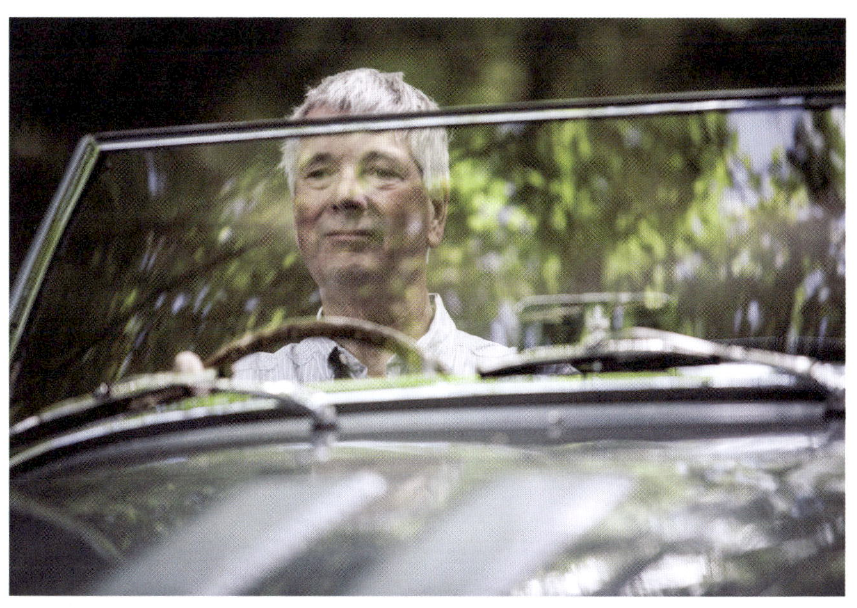

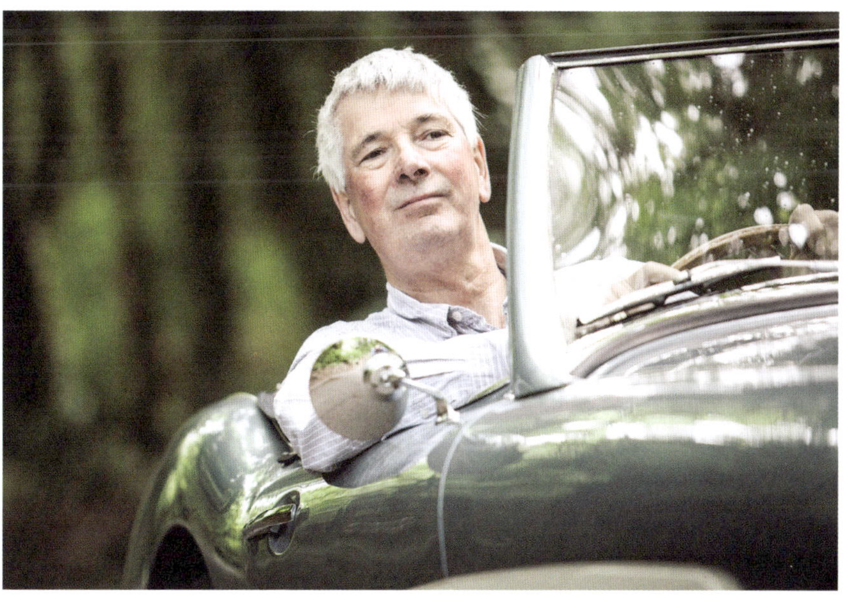

TECHNIQUE

- If the frame itself needs to be sharp, select a small aperture of around f/11. If it needs to be out of focus, select a wider aperture of f/2.8 or f/4.

- The frame should complement the subject and shouldn't be too distracting in terms of design and color.

- The frame doesn't need to be square or rectangular—it could be circular, oval, or even triangular. Think outside the box!

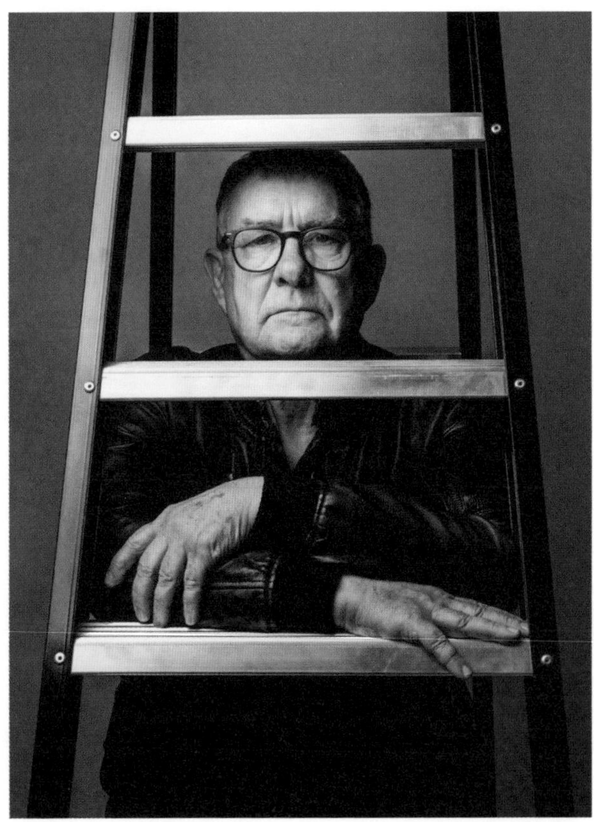

◀ *You can use a frame conceptually by making it relevant to the subject.*

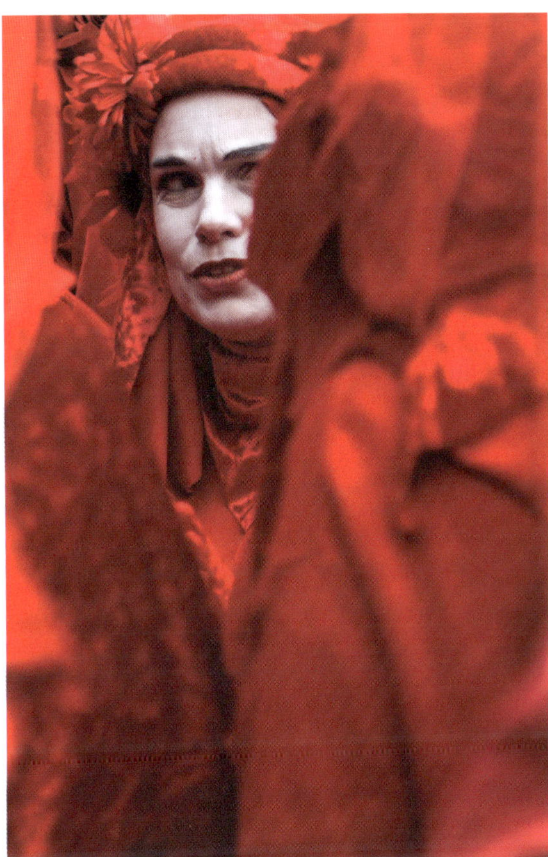

PRO TIP

Think about the lines
of the frame—do they
need to be straight, or
would wonky angles
create a little desirable
tension? A frame at an
unusual angle could
be used to lead the
viewer's eye toward
or away from the main
subject. If you're going
for an angle that's not
straight, exaggerate it a
little to make it obvious
that it's a deliberate
creative choice and not
an error.

FRAMED

We're not talking about picture frames here, rather some kind of frame to place your subject within. Framing (sometimes referred to as sub-framing) is a great way to draw attention to your subject's face—and it can be a fun and quirky addition to a portrait.

This assignment is all about surrounding your subject with different elements. There are several ways you can create a frame: use shadows falling on the face; make the frame part of the concept; choose an object that's relevant to the subject; use windows and doors—these make natural-looking frames; ask the subject to make a frame with their hands; use color (or contrast) to surround the subject.

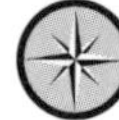

TECHNIQUE

- Shoot in portrait orientation—you don't see many landscape-format magazines!

- Longer focal lengths provide a more flattering facial perspective (the wider the lens, the more the distortion), so a focal length of between 85mm to 135mm is ideal.

- Although it's not an essential feature, the face is always an attention grabber, so think about where you want the eyes, nose, and mouth to be positioned on the cover.

- Leave plenty of space at the top of the frame for the masthead.

- If you have design software such as Adobe InDesign or Affinity Publisher, have fun designing a mocked-up cover.

▶ *The focus is on the food, which is what this fictitious magazine is all about.*

TAKE COVER

Have you ever looked at the image on the cover of a glossy magazine and thought to yourself, "I could do that"? Many of the "big name" portrait photographers started out shooting covers and features for magazines—and many still do—and here's your chance to give it a try for yourself.

There are thousands of magazines published, from general interest to specialist hobbies, so find one that appeals to you and imagine that you've just been commissioned to shoot the cover. Your job is to produce an image that screams "Buy me!" to potential buyers—a front cover that really stands out on the newsstand.

When shooting your editorial cover portrait, remember to leave lots of space around the subject for the art director to crop to their specification (they'll want to add text, thumbnail images, headlines, etc.). Also think about the color and luminosity of the background and the amount of clutter—try to visualize how the designer's text might work with your background.

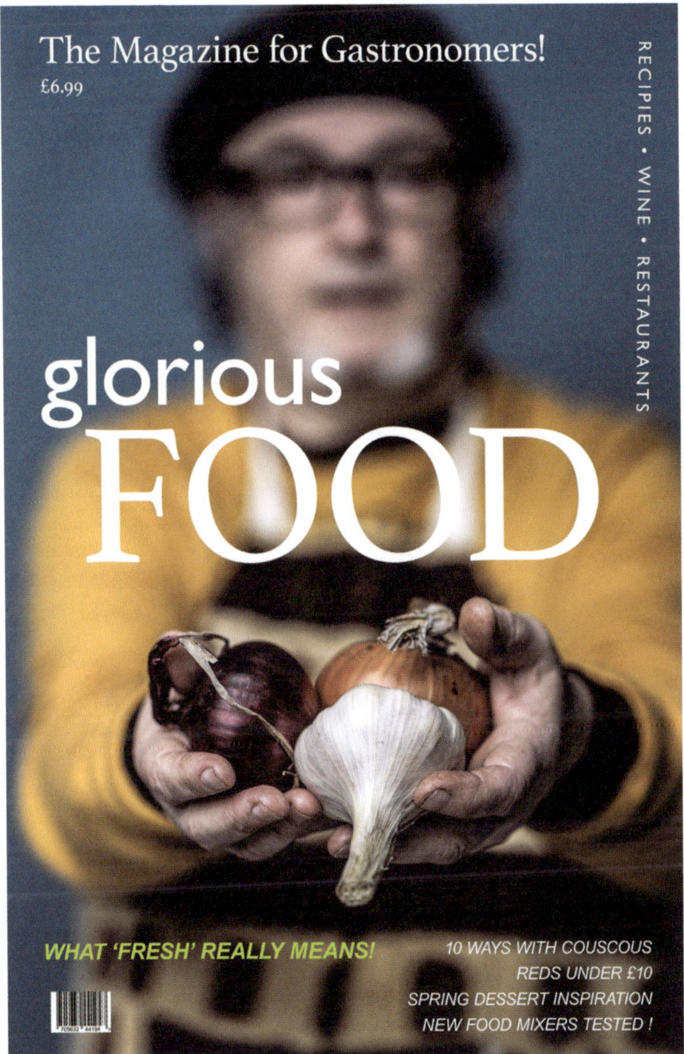

PRO TIP

When shooting for a magazine cover, you need to think about how the photo will work when type is added at the design stage. A super-fast aperture such as f/1.2 will produce a very shallow depth of field and throw great swathes of the frame out of focus, giving the designers plenty of space to place text or thumbnail images. Also, clean images—those devoid of any unnecessary detail or distractions—work best, as magazine covers tend to be busy pages that have to work hard to grab potential readers' attention.

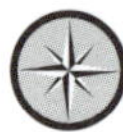
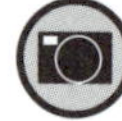

▼ *Even if they're marching, most protestors will pause for a moment to pose for you—and you may even be able to ask them to step aside for a portrait.*

TECHNIQUE

- Look for strong expressions to add emotion to your portrait: humor, anger, sadness, elation, etc.

- You can either ask the person if you can take your picture or just nod toward your camera—most will then pose for you.

- Backgrounds are often distracting so use a wide aperture to isolate your subject.

- Don't be afraid to direct your subject— maybe tell them where to look or how to stand.

- Look for interesting or funny placards—and you get a bonus point if you can link your subject's expression to what's on the sign!

- Rather than just shoot one random protestor, why not turn this into a project and shoot a series of them?

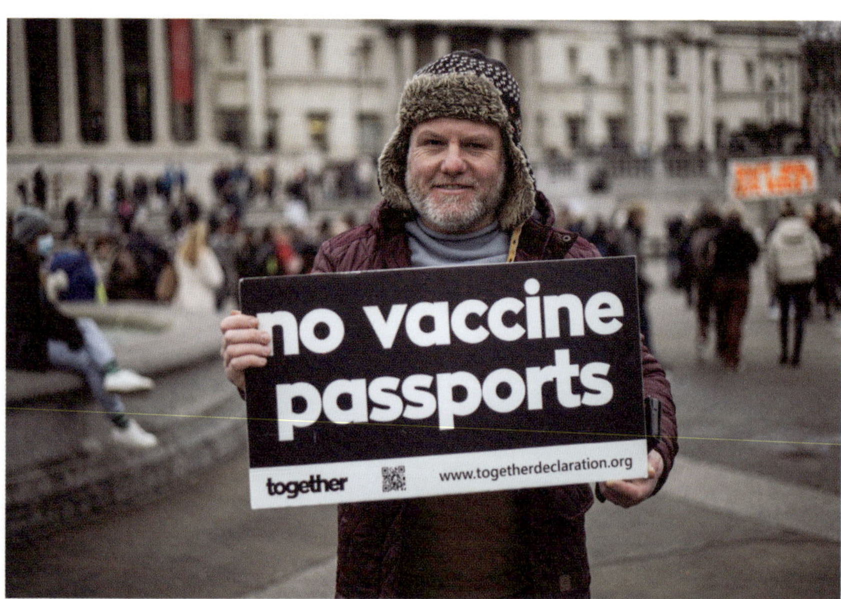

REBEL WITH A CAUSE

In this highly politicized and socially aware world, it's difficult to turn a corner in our towns and cities without encountering people protesting about some issue or other. Sometimes they're in large, organized groups, sometimes you'll find a lone protestor. Either way, they will probably be game to have their portrait taken.

Protestors come in many different guises, but they are often real characters and there's something about them which makes them photogenic. It could be their clothing, the signs they carry, their attitude, or their passion for their cause.

This assignment is all about taking a posed, rather than a candid, portrait. Most protestors are happy to oblige. After all, they want publicity for their cause. This will encourage you to work quickly (protests are often fast-moving events) so you'll need to have your camera set up. Shoot in aperture-priority mode, with an aperture of f/2.8 or wider and a medium-to-high ISO—this combination will allow you to isolate the subject from the background and minimize subject blur and camera shake. The ideal lens is in the 35–50mm range.

PRO TIP

Take care at protests. While most are good-natured and safe, things can quickly change so don't carry lots of gear and always be aware of your surroundings. Always have an escape route in mind and perhaps position yourself close to police officers. If you're concerned for your safety, stay at the edges of the protest so you can make a quick exit if you need to.

ASSIGNMENT JOURNAL

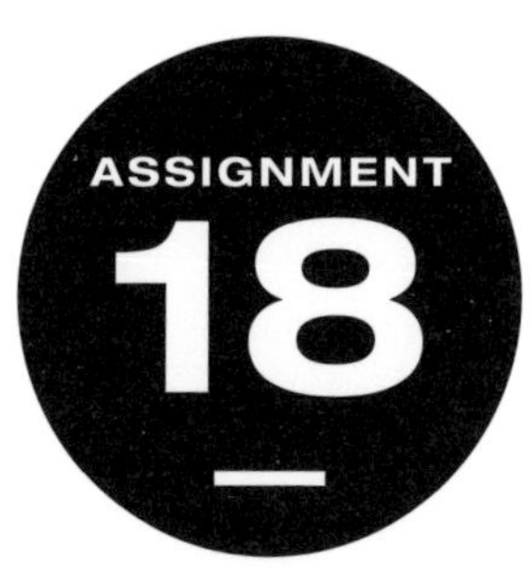

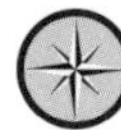

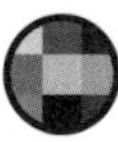

TECHNIQUE

- Try to find a dark and "urban" backdrop—think graffiti, steel shutters, trash in the street, burned-out cars, etc.

- You can use either natural light or flash. If there's not enough ambient light, a speedlight is enough to provide a harsh, directional burst of light.

- High-speed sync (HSS) flash will allow you to select a fast shutter speed to keep the ambient light low, adding to the dark mood.

- Take care if you're in a less-salubrious area—be aware of who's around you and always keep a close eye on your kit.

PRO TIP

Add to the mood with a little extra clarity and texture in post-production (but don't overdo it). You could also add a vignette to help keep the background dark. Look for dimly lit areas and avoid bright sunlight. Some shadow on your subject's face can add to the "gritty" vibe.

CITY LIMITS

Our towns and cities offer great locations for gritty urban portraits. Most have dark alleys, exposed brickwork, iron fire escapes, and graffiti, all perfect for this assignment, which is about capturing a certain mood and conveying a sense of urban darkness. It's as much about the setting as it is about the person.

The object of the exercise isn't necessarily to flatter, it's to produce an atmospheric and edgy portrait, perhaps even with an air of menace. Imagine you're shooting a film noir poster, or the album cover for a punk band—this is the sort of look you should be thinking about. Photographers like Chase Jarvis, Rankin, and Bruce Davidson are worth checking out for inspiration. Basically, you want ATTITUDE!

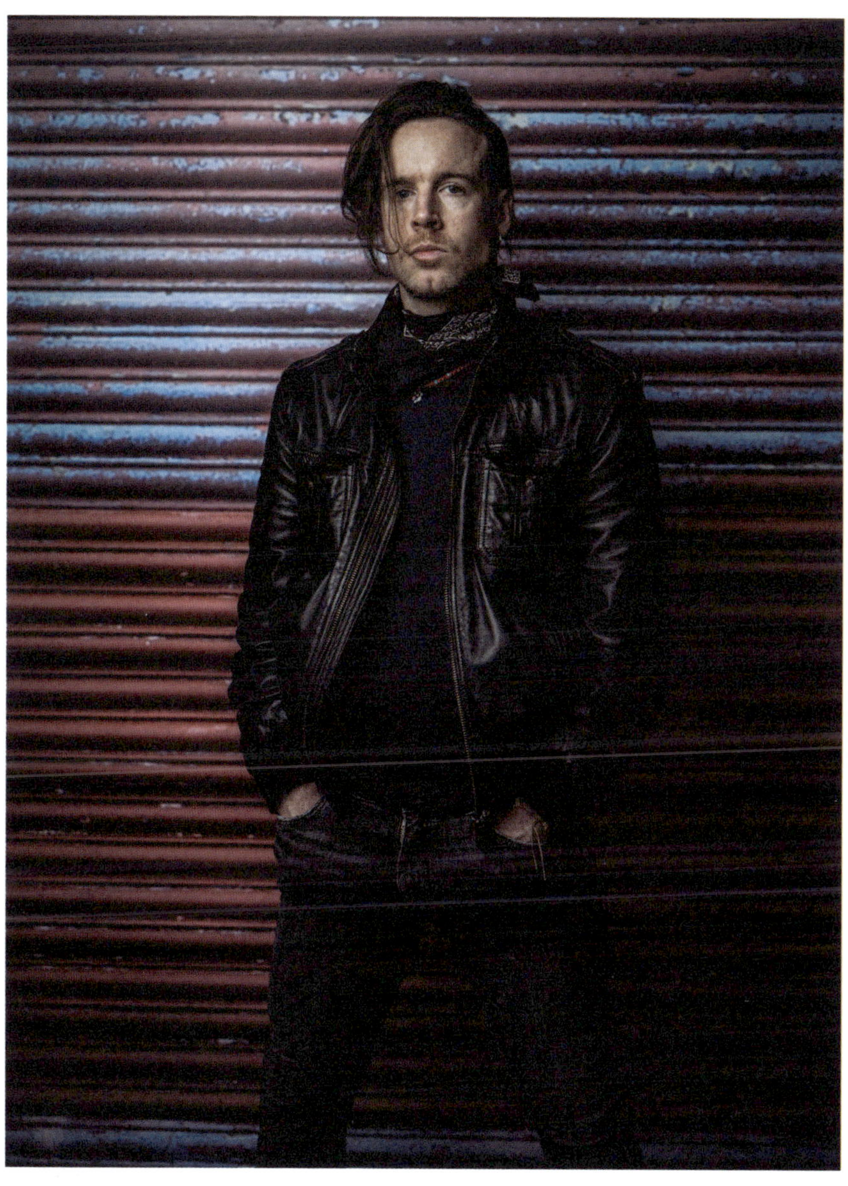

▲ *The steel shutters, the low lighting, and the attitude all contribute to the effect.*

ASSIGNMENT

19

TECHNIQUE

- Look at the subject's body language—when they're looking away from the camera, this becomes even more important. Direct your subject to create a pose that conveys the emotion or mood you're trying to capture, one that is in sync with their appearance and expression.

- There are no hard and fast rules when it comes to creating portraits, so experiment with different techniques and approaches until you find the one that works best for you and your subject.

ASSIGNMENT JOURNAL

PRO TIP

Giving your subject a focal point to look at rather than saying "look over there" will encourage a more purposeful and intense look. Use this technique when storytelling is an important ingredient in your image.

▶ *Who is this man? Why is he standing there smoking a big cigar? What's he thinking? Portraits can ask as many questions as they answer and it can be good to encourage the viewer's mind to do a little work!*

DON'T LOOK NOW

We often see striking portraits in which the subject is deliberately looking away from the camera and we can use this technique to convey feelings of vagueness, mindfulness, thoughtfulness, or even discord. Once we remove eye contact, we think differently about the subject: why are they looking away? What's on their mind?

We're conditioned into thinking that our portrait subjects should generally be looking down the barrel of the lens. Well, in this assignment, they'll be doing the opposite. Portraits where the subject is looking away from the camera can be evocative and powerful, sometimes bringing a feeling of mystery, intrigue, or tension.

Consider the angle of the subject's face and experiment with different angles to find the one that works best for the vibe you're trying to create. Use the off-camera look to build a narrative based on the visual clues within the frame, perhaps making a connection with what the subject is looking at.

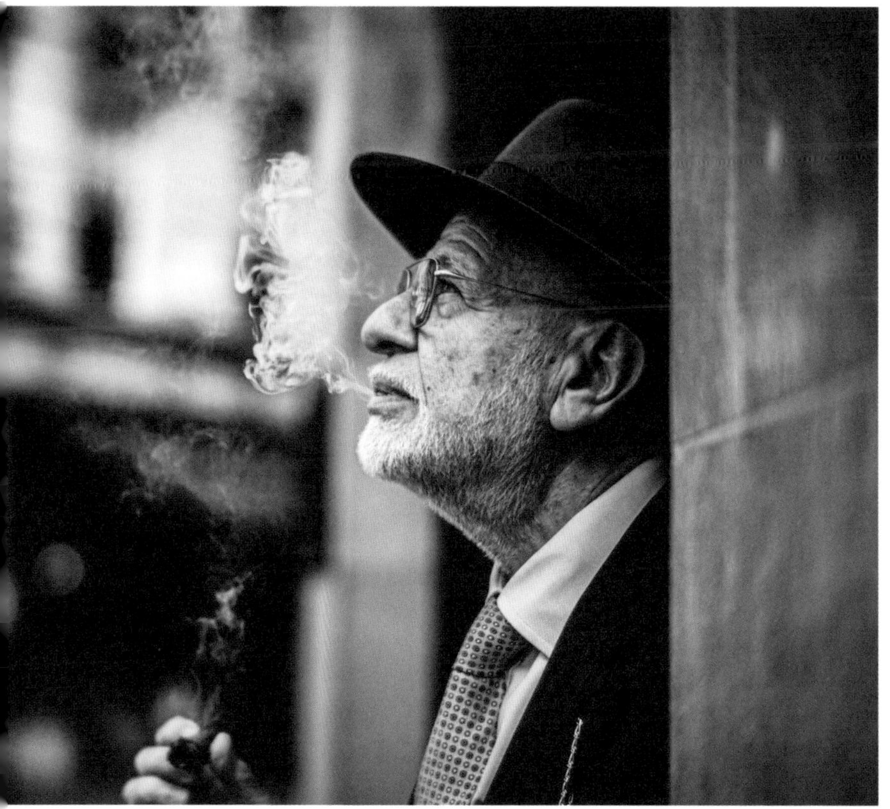

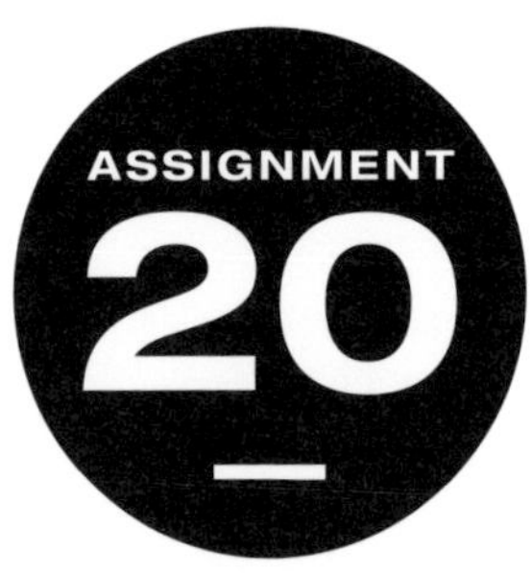

TECHNIQUE

- Crop in camera rather than in post-production. This way the image will always feel more "designed." It also means that you'll more easily be able to create an out-of-focus background, thus minimizing distractions. A bonus with this approach is that image quality and file size will be unaffected.

- Crop above the hair line, leaving the forehead unaffected, and make sure you focus on the eyes with pinpoint accuracy.

- This technique works best with direct eye contact but it's worth experimenting with different poses.

ASSIGNMENT JOURNAL

PRO TIP

Consider the aspect ratio you're using. With a wide aspect ratio such as 16:9, the face might look squashed; with a square aspect ratio (1:1), it could look elongated. Balance is the key.

▶ *Direct eye contact combined with this crop can create powerful portraits which work well for suited business types.*

OFF WITH THEIR HEADS

Rules are made to be broken. When we're learning photography, we're invariably told to make sure we don't "cut" someone's head off, and that's often a good rule of thumb. Sometimes, however, by chopping the top of your subject's head off, you'll get a more intimate and impactful portrait that draws the viewer into the subject's eyes more effectively.

We often see images cropped for dramatic effect in newspapers and magazines, the intention being to create more attention-grabbing articles.

In this assignment, you'll deliberately chop off the top of your subject's head. This is all about balance—crop the head too high and it will look like a mistake, crop too low and the frame will look unbalanced. A good rule of thumb is to ensure the eyes are placed roughly one-third of the way down from the top of the frame.

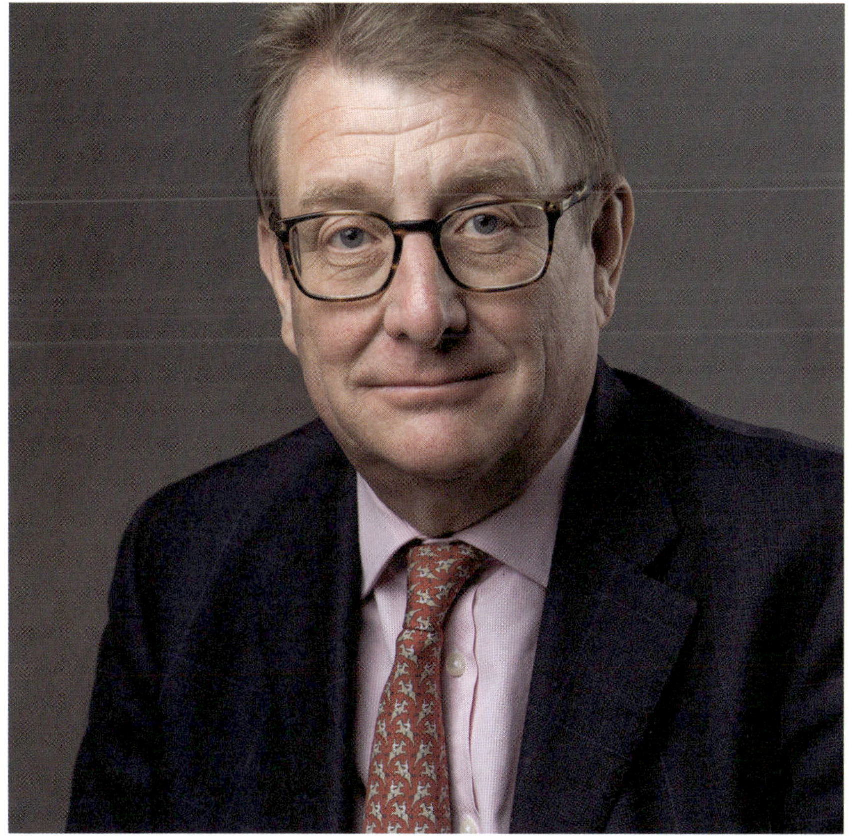

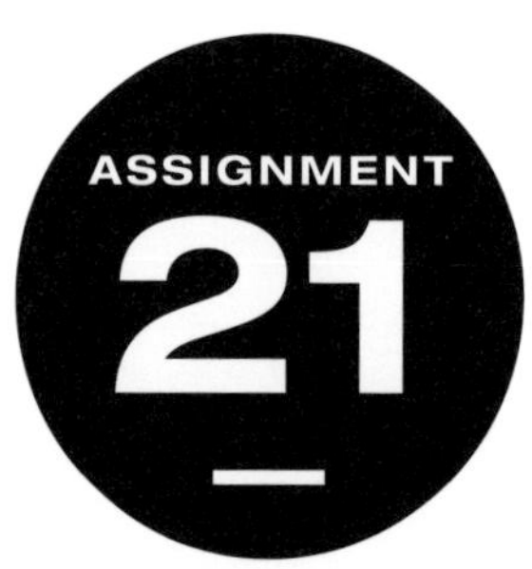

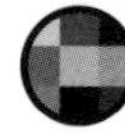

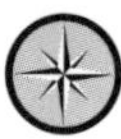

TECHNIQUE

- To really get into the Bailey style, shoot in black and white, which will help evoke that classic 1960s look.

- Encourage your subject to be free with their gestures and expressions.

- Compose with a 1:1 aspect ratio in mind. Many cameras feature a square aspect ratio mode. If not, visualize the square frame while shooting and crop in post-production.

- Try doing this with your friends to create a fun mini project.

- A black border around the frame, added in post-production, helps reinforce the feeling of confinement within the square.

▶ *Bailey liked to create a feeling of constraint or confinement, with his subjects seemingly needing to burst out of the edges of the frame.*

BE BAILEY

David Bailey was a legendary photographer in the 1960s, '70s, and '80s, who had a distinctive portrait style which brought about a refreshing revolution in the fashion industry. He eschewed the cumbersome medium-format camera on a tripod in favor of a more maneuverable handheld 35mm model, allowing him to move around and constantly direct his subjects.

As a portrait photographer, his iconic *Box of Pin-Ups* project in 1965 saw him first using what became his trademark style of shooting portraits, with harsh lighting against a white background with the intention of totally isolating his subjects, often cropping them into impossibly tight compositions.

This is a great style for you to experiment with—and it's easy. You just need one light (even the anglepoise lamp from your desk would work), a plain wall and a willing subject. Find a harsh, directional light source, ideally a single flash shot through a small umbrella or beauty dish, placed to one side of the subject at around 45°. You'll need a plain background—ideally white—which could simply be a painted wall.

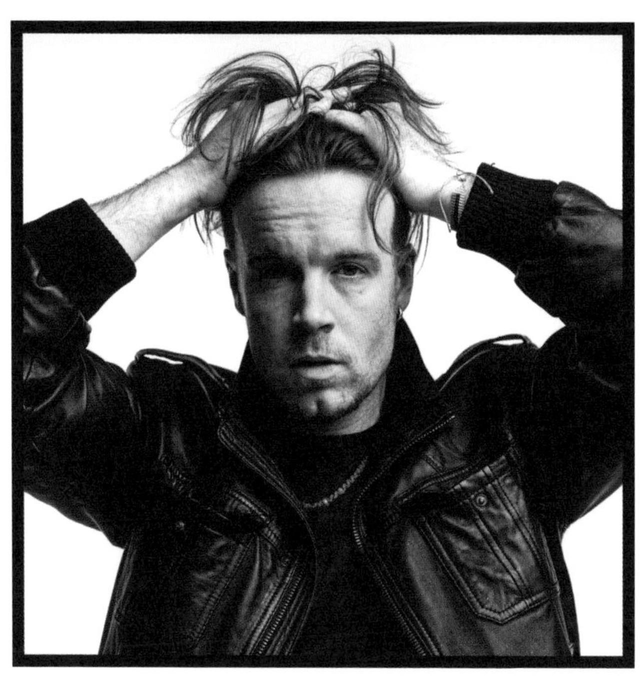

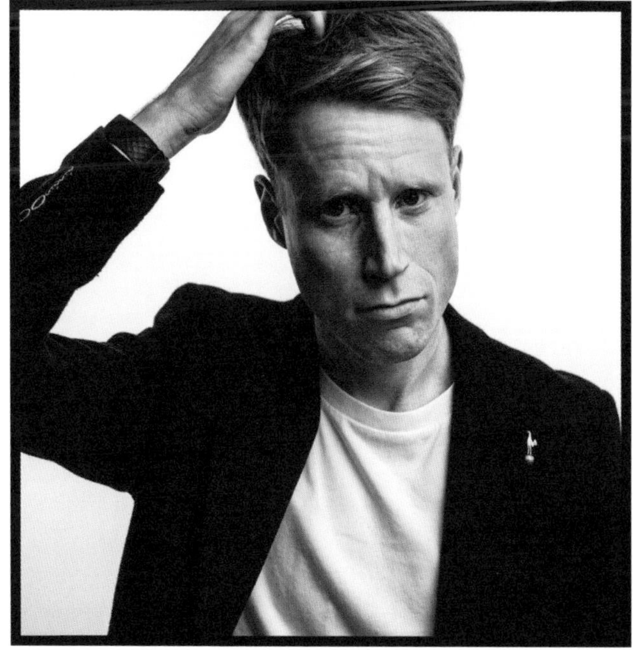

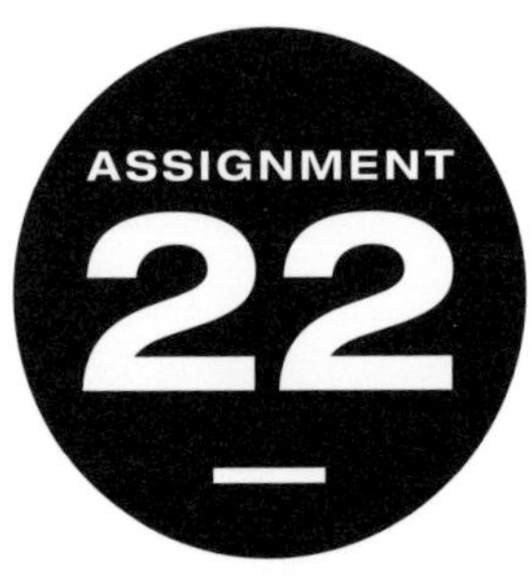

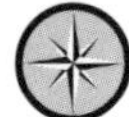

TECHNIQUE

- Find people who look as though they may have an interesting story to tell—you should find plenty of such characters in any city or town center.

- It's essential to build rapport, so talk to your subjects, ask them about their lives, and listen to their stories. This will help you build a strong connection, inevitably leading to a stronger portrait.

- Consider what makes your subject interesting. Is it their clothes, tattoos, hair, overall look, surroundings, attitude? This detail is essential in capturing the essence of the person.

- Shooting with a wide aperture will draw attention to the face and help eliminate cluttered backgrounds.

- Respect people's privacy—if it's a "no," it's a no.

▶ *Sometimes, a prop (in this case, the camera) will help tell a person's story. Try to find out what's important to someone and make that part of their image.*

PRO TIP

If you're planning to publish your project either online or in print, plan what you want to include in your captions to add context and a little narrative sparkle to the photos. For example, you might want to ask the people you photograph for their first name and a quote about their life, the sort of day they're having, or their view of the world.

THE HUMANS OF ...

Brandon Stanton's ongoing *Humans of New York* project started as a blog before being published as a best-selling photobook. His project features portraits of strangers he comes across in New York—he finds someone who looks interesting, asks them for a portrait, and jots down a few notes.

In this assignment, choose an area and aim to capture the spirit and the character of the people who live and work there. By following Stanton's lead, this can become much more than a series of simple street portraits—a living, breathing ongoing project. For more tips on taking this kind of picture, read Assignment #9 before you start work on your project. This is the perfect assignment to turn into a book, zine (a self-published magazine), or blog about the people where you live.

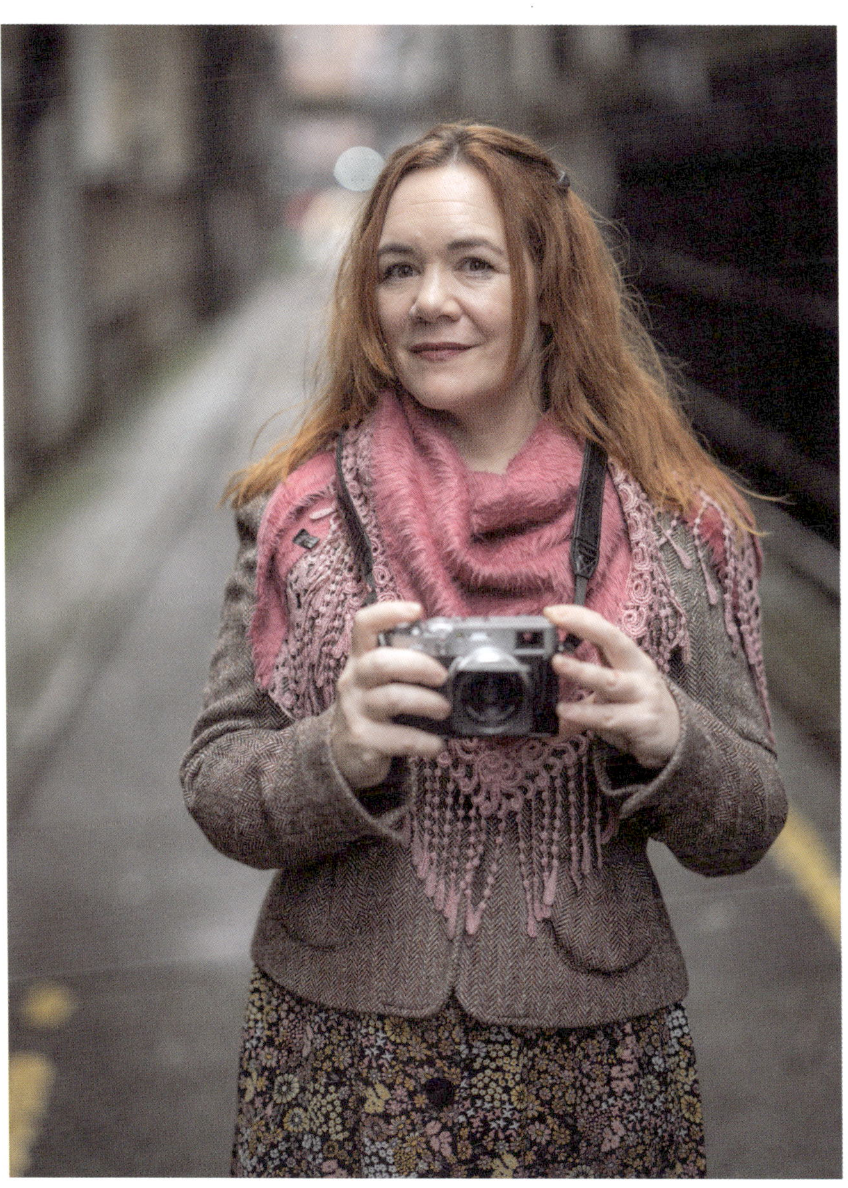

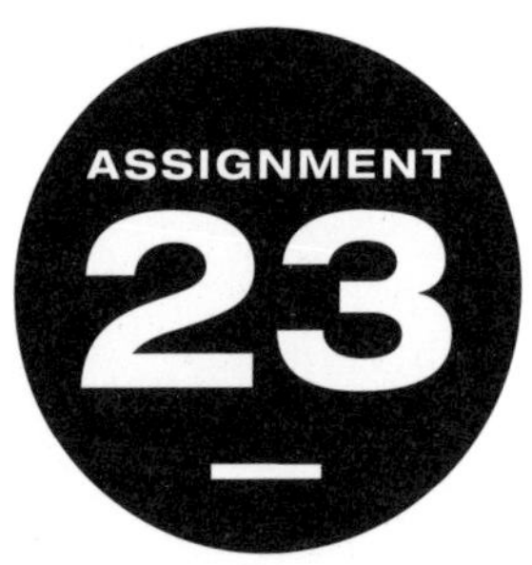

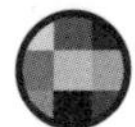

ASSIGNMENT JOURNAL

____

____

____

____

____

____

____

____

____

TECHNIQUE

- A bright but overcast day is ideal for window-lit portraits. Light clouds act as a giant softbox, producing a flattering, diffused light, especially at the beginning or end of the day.

- Vary the distance between the subject and the window to control the intensity of the light (and the contrast).

- If the window light is too harsh, drape a translucent material such as a net curtain (or a diffusing panel, if you have one) over the window to soften the effect.

- Switch off any artificial light sources and, if the room has more than one window, close the other curtains or blinds.

- Think about the temperature of the light and adjust your white balance accordingly (the temperature will often move from cool to neutral to warm as the day progresses). Also remember that the color of the walls or floor may affect your white balance.

- Avoid the temptation to use fill-in flash, which can kill the soft atmosphere. Instead, find the biggest window you can.

PRO TIP

Avoid the "deadeye" look and make sure your subject's eyes have catchlights (the reflection of the light source)—this may need a small re-positioning of the head to get the catchlights right. If there's too much contrast, a reflector will bounce some light into the unlit side of your subject.

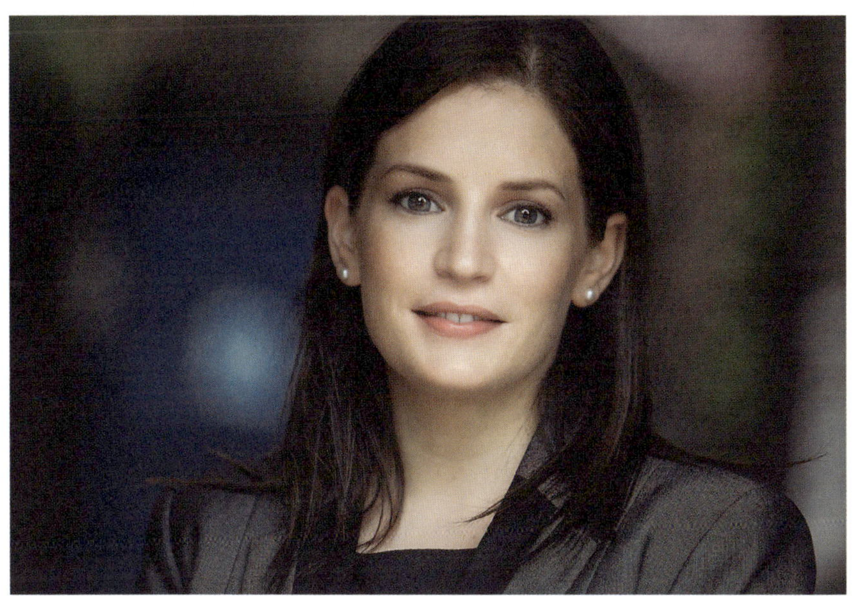

SOFTLY DOES IT

Natural daylight from a window is one of the softest, most flattering, and delightful sources of light a portrait photographer can ask for—and there's always plenty of it around, wherever you are. Window light wraps around the skin, giving it a lovely luminance and producing a very flattering result.

Think of the window as nature's giant softbox. Like using any softbox, the bigger the better, and think of the positioning of your subject in relation to the window as being your major lighting control. North-facing windows often work best for this because the sun never shines directly through them.

Your assignment is to shoot a posed window-lit portrait. Shoot close (head and shoulders is ideal) to show the lovely effects of the soft light on the skin.

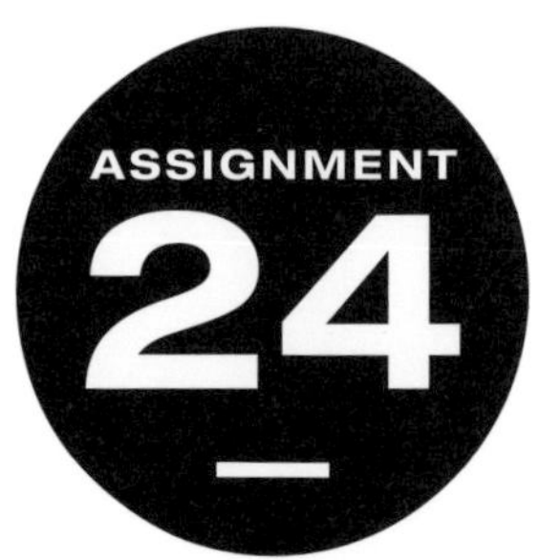

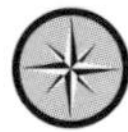

TECHNIQUE

- Choose a location that links to your subject's sport, such as a tennis court, football field, or running track.

- Shoot from low angles to make the athlete appear more powerful or shoot from above to create a more dynamic image.

- If your subject is moving, use as fast a shutter speed as possible—or maybe try panning using a slow shutter speed of around 1/15 sec. or 1/30 sec.

THE SPORTRAIT

Whether they're playing their sport or simply posing for you, athletes can make great portrait subjects, as they usually exude an energy for their sport—and are often surrounded by interesting props.

Your challenge for this assignment is to convey your athlete's sporting personality and passion from a static pose (it's a portrait, not an action shot). This portrait could be a close-up or a wider view, such as a footballer with the bleachers in the background. It could be shot using a friend who is a keen amateur, or your subject could be a professional athlete.

Ask someone to specifically pose for you, as this gives you the perfect opportunity to direct them. Pose them against the best background and in the best possible light; direct their pose and expression and organize any props you think will add to the portrait (they could be holding something like a football, or they could be surrounded by paraphernalia related to their sport).

PRO TIP

Pay attention to details. Something as simple as having your subject hold a cheap football could destroy the credibility of the image. Research and a reasonable working knowledge of the sport will help you to better engage with your subject and ensure the image has the right feel.

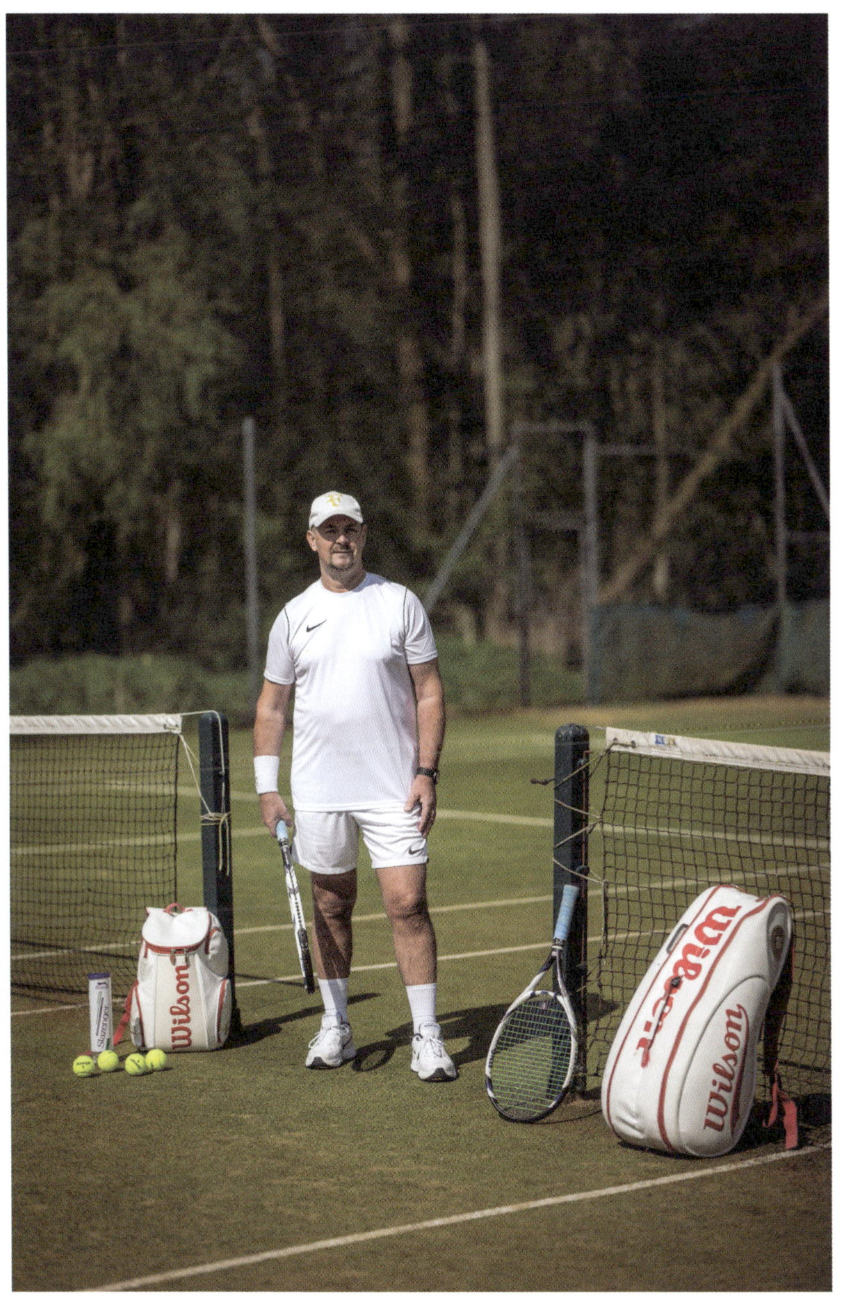

▲ *Use as many props as are appropriate for your "sportrait"—context is everything.*

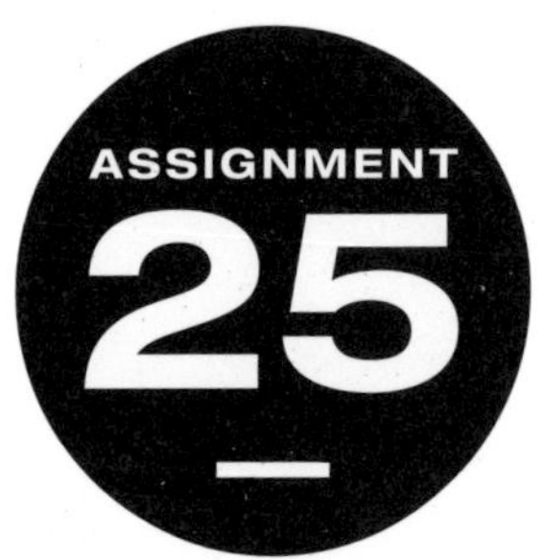

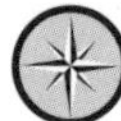

TECHNIQUE

- If you're shooting indoors, you may encounter several different light sources, all with different temperatures. In this case, consider shooting in black and white.

- Before shooting, make sure everything looks clean and tidy and that (as far as possible) everything in the background is relevant to the shot.

- Compile a comprehensive shot list to make sure you get everything and take lots of shots with as many variations and poses as possible.

- Watch out for highly reflective surfaces that could distract from the subject. Take a few test shots and check the results on the back of the camera. If using flash with modeling lamps, switch these on and evaluate the effects of the lighting.

UP THE WORKERS

In this assignment, you'll be shooting someone in their place of work. Whether they're working outside in a public place or inside their own place of work, people engaged in their craft or profession make engaging subjects for portraits.

There are two ways of approaching this: you can either shoot someone you come across during your day—for example, a shopkeeper or a police officer—or you can take a more planned approach by contacting your subject in advance and asking if you can photograph them at work.

Choose people with interesting jobs that will make strong images, such as a traditional carpenter, a cheesemaker, a chef, and so on. Those with outdoor jobs are usually easier to photograph because you won't need to worry too much about lighting—just remember to avoid the harsh midday sun when planning your shoot.

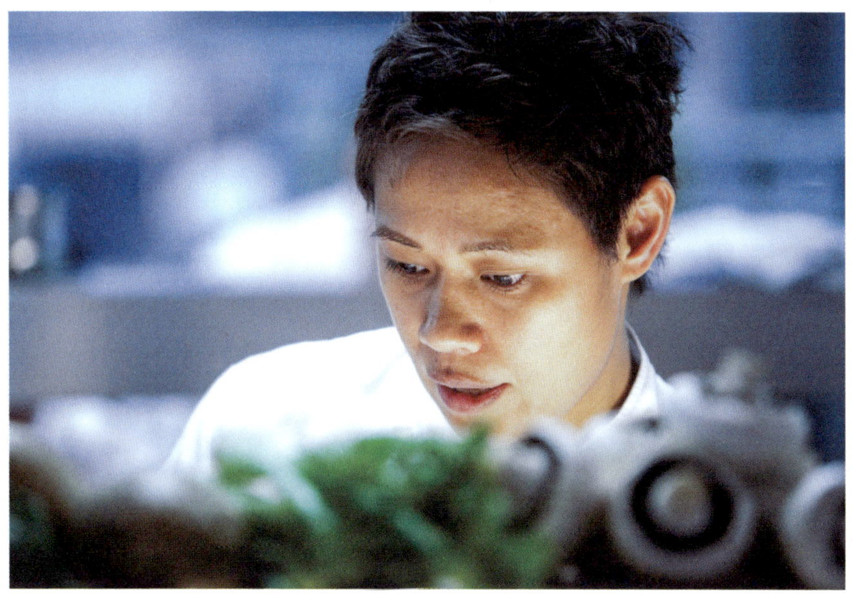

▲ *The out-of-focus vegetables provide a nice lead-in to the portrait of the chef.*

ASSIGNMENT JOURNAL

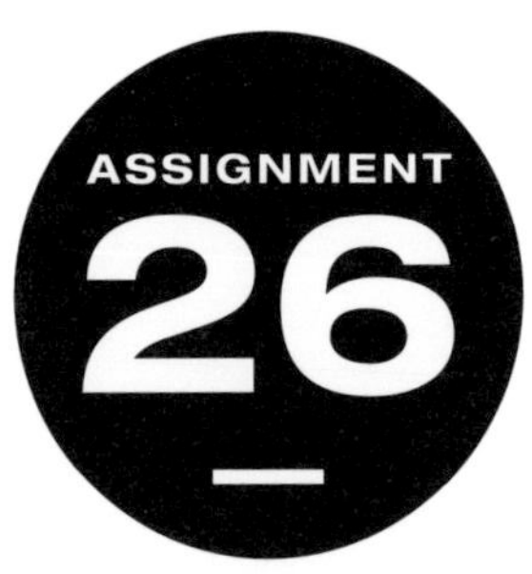

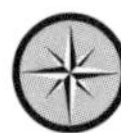

TECHNIQUE

- The portrait is the anchor shot for your photo-essay and should encapsulate the essence of the story. It could be a close-up or a longer view taking in the context of the background.

- Aim for between four and eight supporting images, each sufficiently different and each contributing to the story in a different way.

- If you're struggling to know where to begin, try leading the viewer chronologically through the story, following a natural sequence of events.

- Aim for visual consistency—the images should all look like they belong together. Aim for a similar aesthetic such as consistent color palette, aspect ratio, and any post-production treatment (color grading, high-contrast effects, etc.).

- Take far more pictures than you think you need and try different compositions, angles, viewpoints, etc. It's often difficult to revisit a shoot, and more pictures give you more options.

PRO TIP

Ask for feedback—what might seem like a clear and logical story to you may not be so obvious to others. Try to find someone who's familiar with the story or situation and can give you constructive critique, not necessarily about the technical merits of the images but about how you are telling the story.

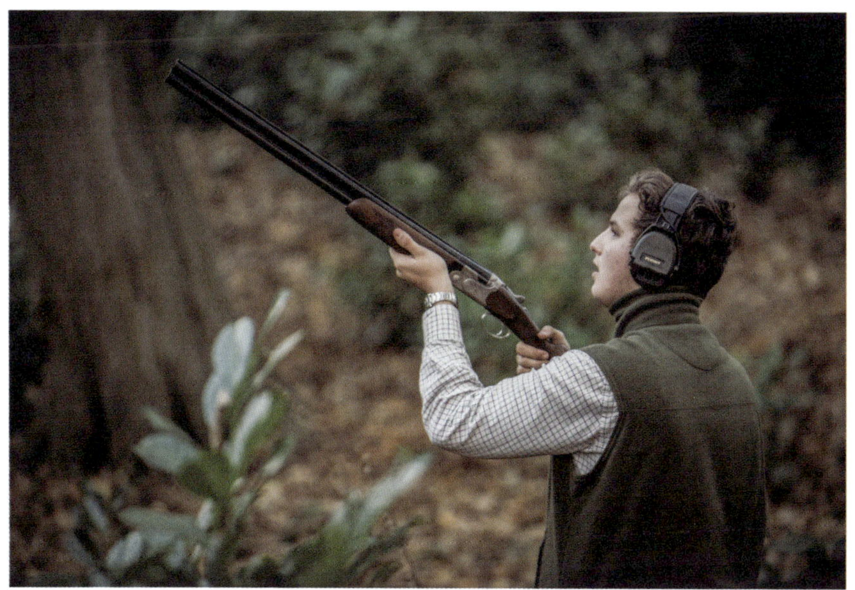

A BIGGER PICTURE

A portrait can sometimes be a part of a bigger picture, used to help tell a story, even though it's not necessarily the story itself. For example, imagine you were shooting a photo-essay about life in food markets—you would probably include shots of the buildings, wide shots showing the ambience, close-ups of the food, and portraits of the market traders. As these vendors are such an important aspect of market life, such portraits would be a key part of the narrative.

This assignment is a portrait-led photo-essay, and you'll need to get creative and develop a short story. Just remember to make the portrait the star of the show. Don't overthink this—your essay could be as simple as telling the story of a family day out by the seaside or of a colorful local event.

Once you've chosen a concept for your story, you'll need to storyboard your idea— think of what pictures you need and how they might "flow" in the right sequence. You could sketch this sequence out, comic-style, or you could just make a chronological list of the pictures you think you need.

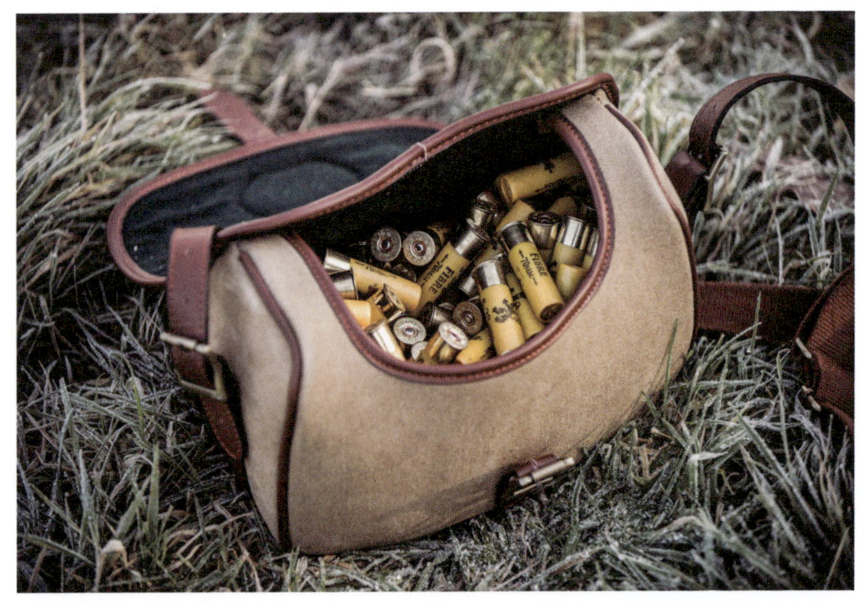

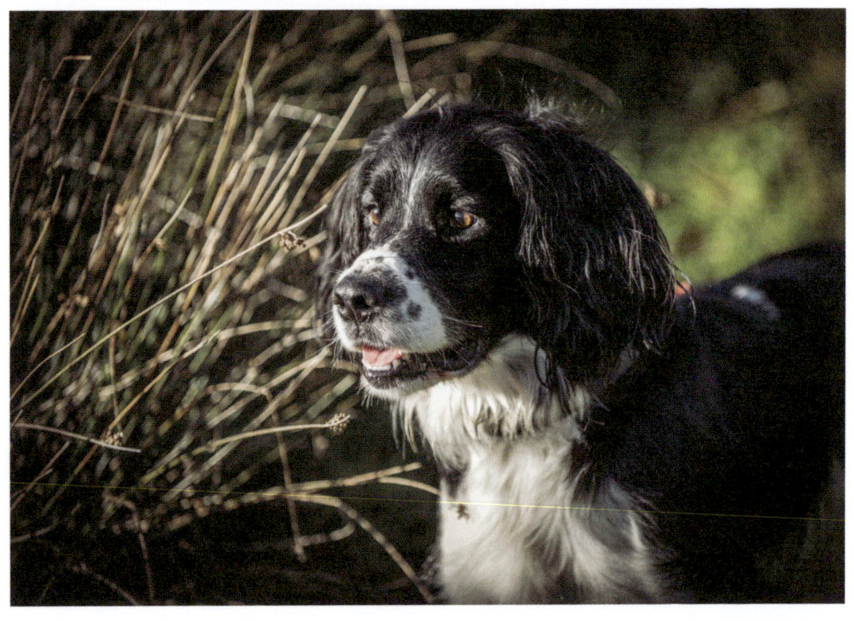

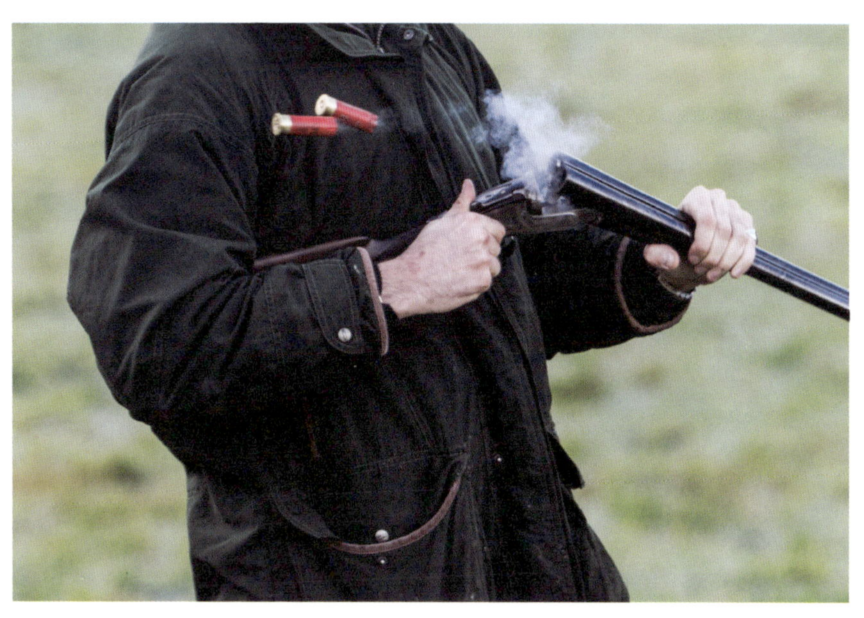

ASSIGNMENT JOURNAL

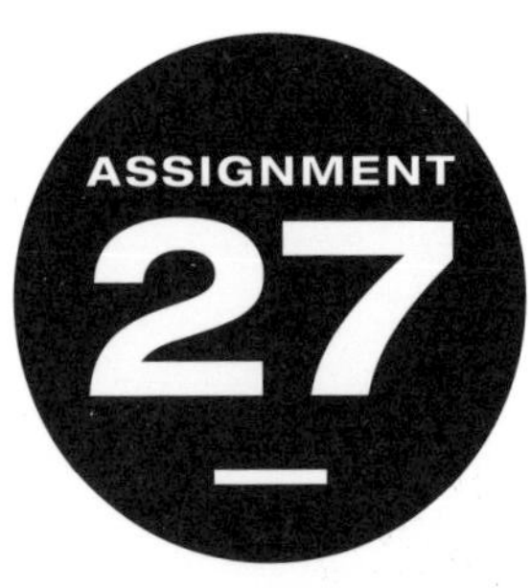

TECHNIQUES

- Generally, the longer the lens, the more flattering the effect on the subject's face.

- Bear in mind that wider lenses distort facial features, especially when shot close-up.

- Remember that choosing the right focal length is just one factor in creating great portraits—lighting, composition, and posing are other essential elements to consider.

SHORT, MEDIUM, LONG

Portrait photography is usually associated with medium telephoto lenses—85mm to 135mm is thought to be ideal. But in this assignment, you're going to experiment with different focal lengths to explore the possibilities of different looks and perspectives.

You'll take the same portrait from roughly the same position with three different focal lengths, using either prime lenses or a zoom. So that you're comparing like with like, shoot each portrait at a similar aperture.

Need to include some background context? Go wide. Looking for some lovely bokeh? 85mm is ideal. Somewhere in the middle? The "nifty fifty" (or thereabouts) is your friend. Here are three options for you to try:

- 85mm: this is probably the "sweet spot" focal length for portraits, providing a flattering perspective and allowing you to get a shallow depth of field. Good for head-and-shoulders shots as well as three-quarter-length portraits.
- 40–55mm: often referred to as the "standard" lens, this is an evergreen option for portraits. It provides a natural perspective that's not too wide or too narrow. It can also be a good choice for full-body portraits.
- 24–28mm: use this when the background adds useful context or when you need a little drama. The wider zoom range means that it's more difficult to get an out-of-focus background.

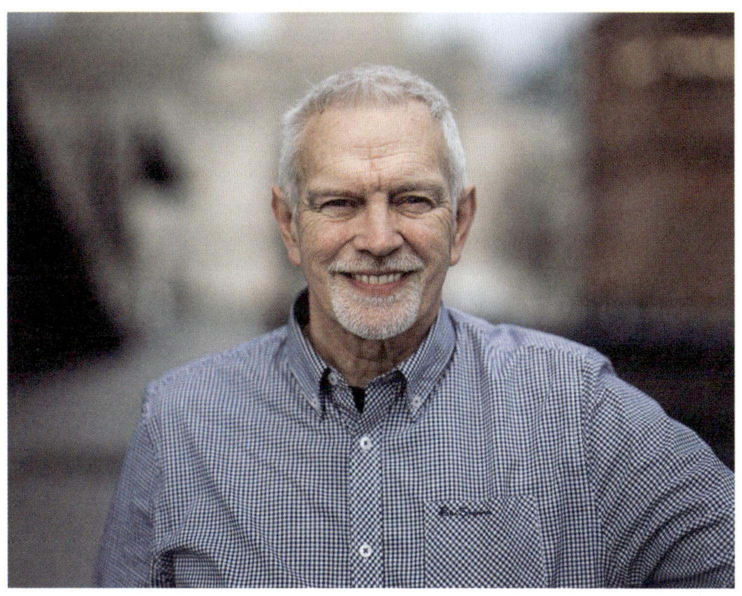

▲ At 85mm, the subject is well separated from the background and the facial features are well proportioned.

▼ At 40mm, the background has a bigger part to play, and the viewpoint feels more natural.

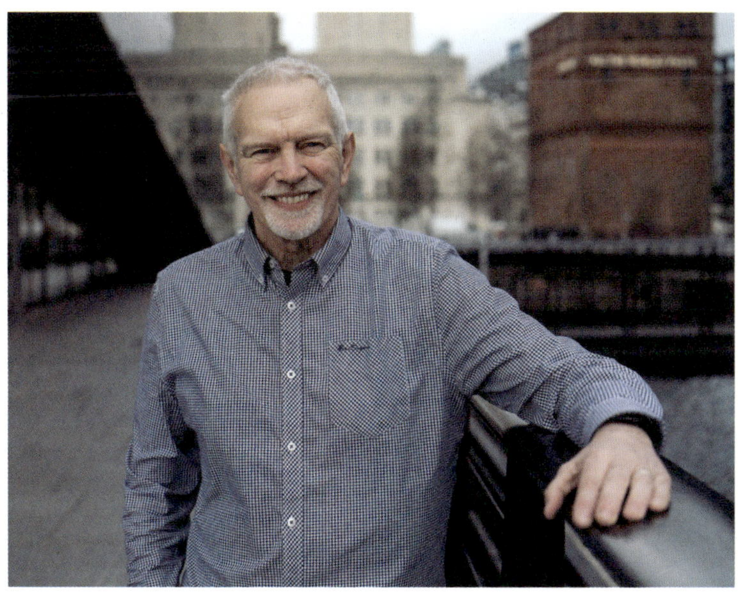

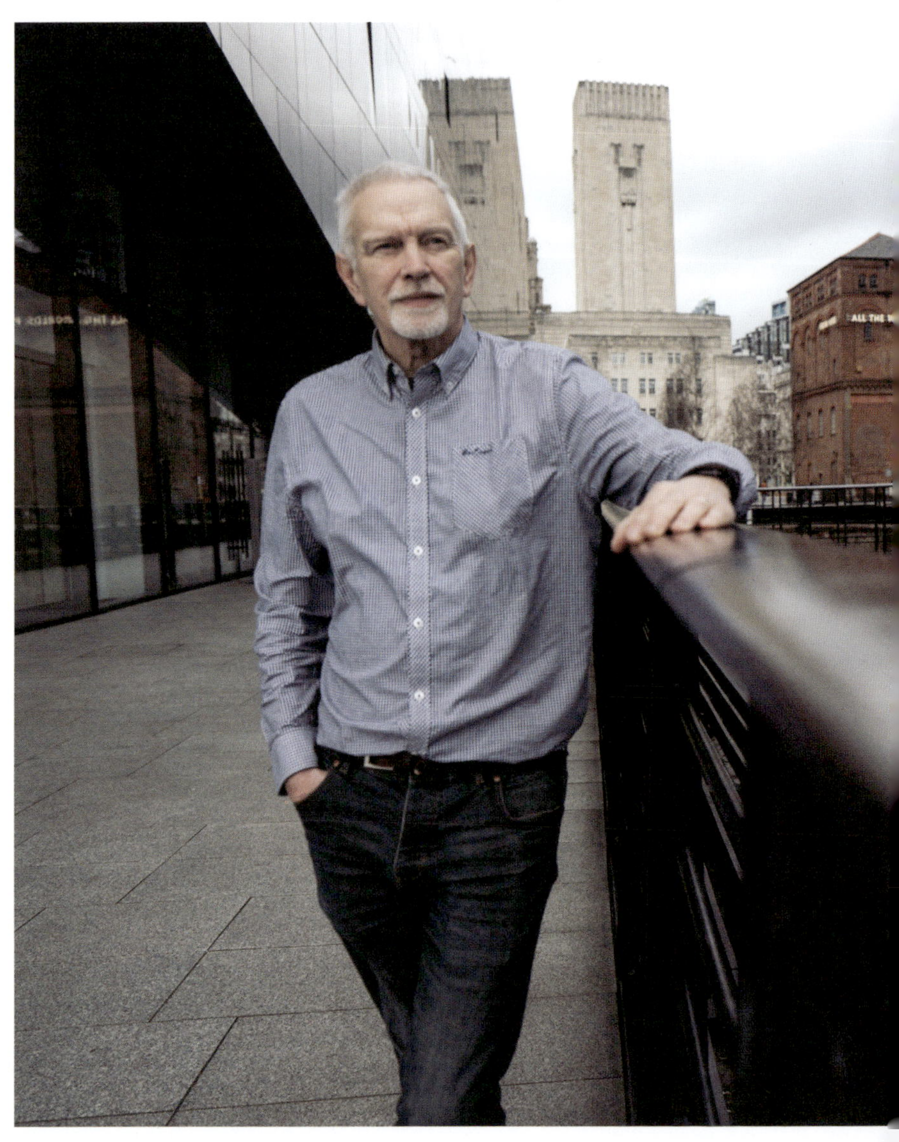

▲ *The 28mm option brings a very different feel to the portrait, making the background a much more important part of the frame.*

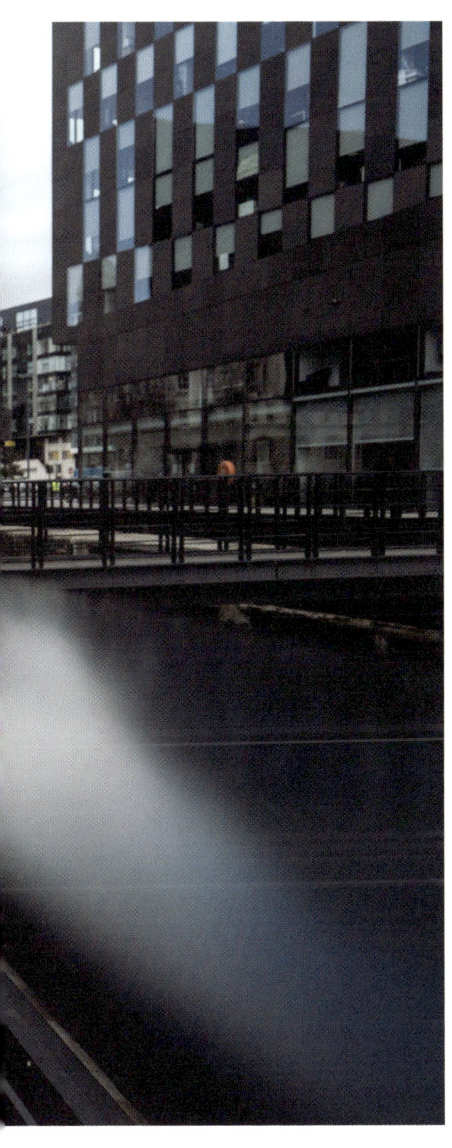

ASSIGNMENT JOURNAL

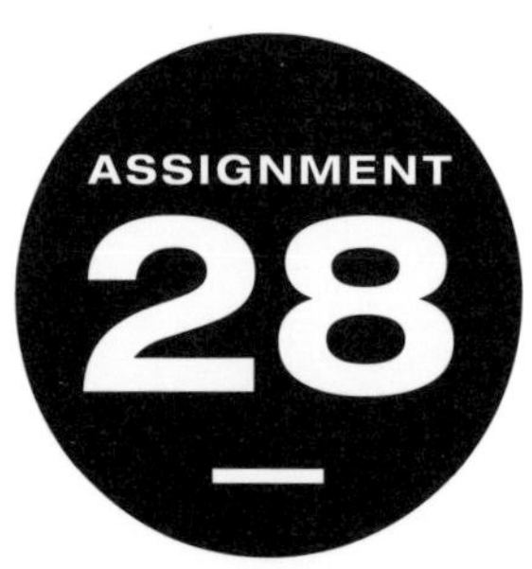

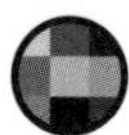

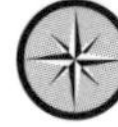

TECHNIQUE

- Don't feel you have to fit out your home studio with lots of expensive kit—you can create stunning portraits with the most basic of setups.

- Switch off any room lights or lamps when you're shooting—this will allow you to control the light on the subject more effectively while avoiding any white balance issues caused by having multiple light sources with different color temperatures.

SET UP A HOME STUDIO

The great thing about shooting in your own home is that you can experiment with different lighting setups, backdrops, and props to find what works best for you, with no time pressure and no studio hire charges. You don't need the photographic equivalent of Abbey Road to make this work and you can set up your home studio in the smallest of spaces.

THE PROCESS

To create your own home studio:

1 Find a suitable space. It doesn't need to be big, and it can be temporary, like the back of your kitchen. Neutral-colored walls are best to avoid unwanted color casts.

2 Make sure you have the essential equipment: camera, lens, and light source (additional lighting, a light meter, tripod, backdrop, and other gear can come later).

3 You'll need a backdrop. Collapsible backgrounds are relatively cheap and can be hung from a picture hook. Alternatively, drape a plain sheet or piece of fabric over the curtain rail. If your space has plain light walls to start with, you're good to go.

You can set up your studio space to take portraits of friends or family—or even to start a small portrait photography business (lots of established photographers have started just like this). And you don't need lots of gear—one light is fine to start with (see Assignment #6), along with a camera and one lens.

For this assignment, you'll find some space in your home (or workplace) and set up a basic portrait studio. Many other assignments in this book would work perfectly well with a small make-do studio space so all you have to do now is find a friend or family member to model for you and away you go.

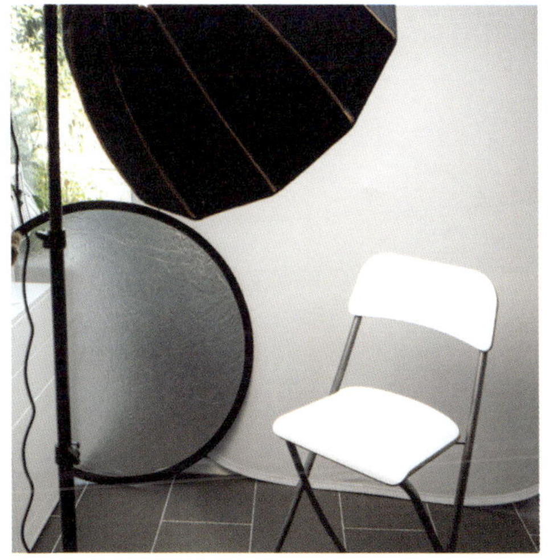

◀ *A basic setup is all you need, and you could do this with one light (which could be an inexpensive continuous light like this one), a reflector, and a plain background such as a bed sheet. A setup like this one won't cost much and can give a professional-looking result.*

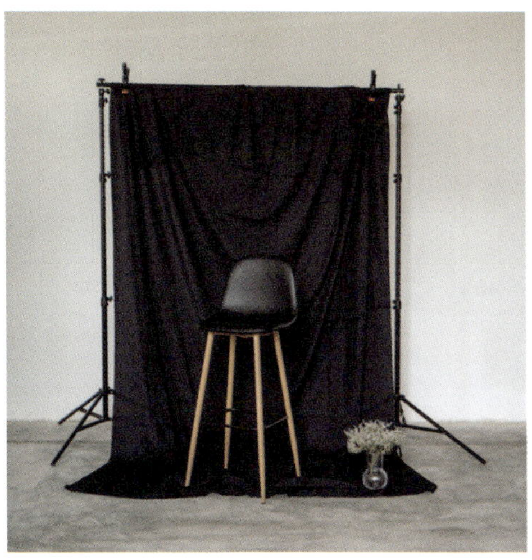

◀ *Alternatively, you can do this just using a big window with indirect light.*

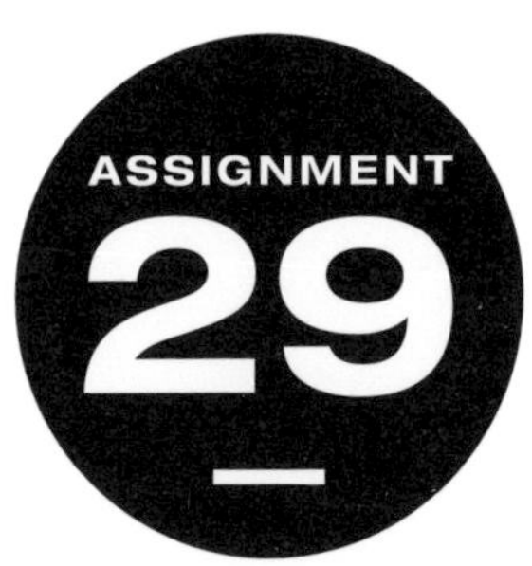

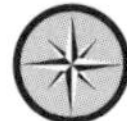

TECHNIQUE

- These events can be very crowded and cluttered so take care to separate your subject from the background, either by differences in color, contrast, or aperture/focus.

- If your subject is wearing a particularly interesting or extravagant outfit, you'll probably want a full body shot so shoot with a wideangle lens. Just be aware of possible distortion if shooting at 24mm or wider, as it tends to be very unflattering.

- A small flash is often handy to make bold colors pop—the built-in flash on many cameras should be fine for this.

- Take your time—they're probably not rushing off anywhere.

PRO TIP

Get some business cards printed—they're not only for professionals! These can be produced quickly and cheaply, and you'll find that a card gives you instant credibility as a photographer. You don't need to give away lots of personal information, just your name and a method of contact (your Instagram handle, for example), and possibly one of your best images on the back.

ALL DRESSED UP

Revivals, steampunk festivals, re-enactments, pride parades . . . there are lots of events where people really dress up for the occasion, and they're usually keen to have their picture taken. Events with a retro or vintage twist are perfect, as people really dress up and are surrounded by interesting props you can incorporate into the background. But this is no ordinary picture—the object of the exercise is to take a posed portrait that captures the essence of the event.

If you're new to asking complete strangers for a portrait, this is a great introduction, as people generally expect—and want—to have their picture taken at certain events. Approach your subject with a smile and confidently ask if you can take their portrait—they'll almost certainly say yes. It's useful if you have some images to show them, even if it's just an Instagram feed on your smartphone. Occasionally, people will turn you down, though this is the exception and not the norm. We all hate rejection, but you must put it behind you and quickly move on to someone else.

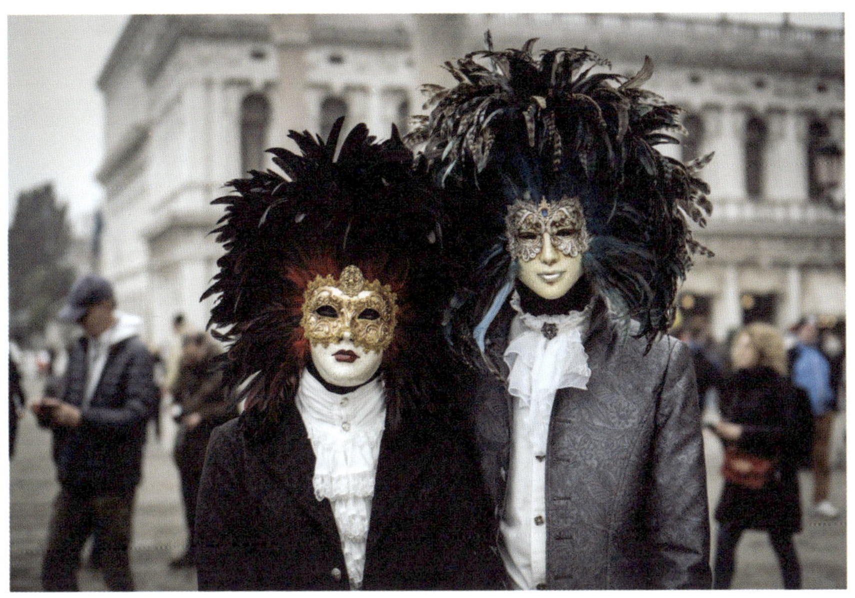

▲ *If people look like this, they expect to be photographed!*

▼ *The portrait doesn't need to be a close-up—why not include some background context to add a sense of place?*

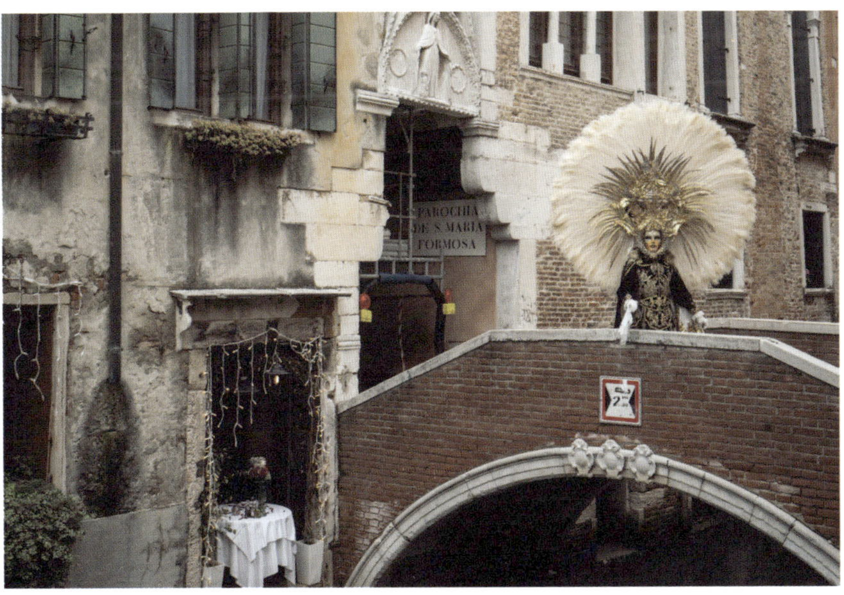

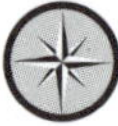

TECHNIQUE

- Use a wide lens. A focal length of 24–35mm, with 28mm being the perfect choice, will help create intimacy.

- Shoot with a flash if you feel you can (although this isn't essential). This will bring a harsh and gritty feel to the shot, exposing every flaw, just as Gilden would do.

- Use a fast shutter speed to freeze the moment, as you and your subject are likely to be moving. Aim for 1/125 sec. or faster.

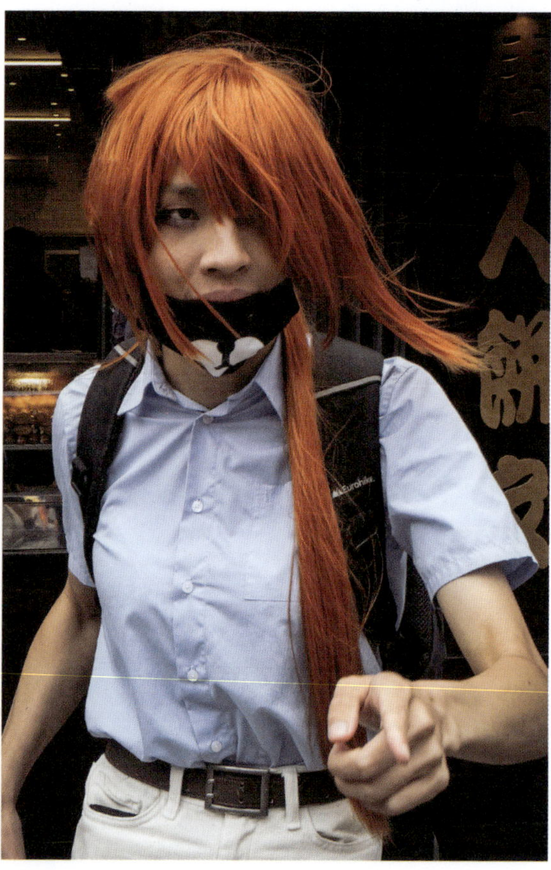

◄ *Take your picture and move on. People may be curious but are rarely hostile. Just avoid quiet places and dark alleys!*

GILDENESQUE

You couldn't call New York street photographer Bruce Gilden a shy person.
His in-your-face style has been referred to as intrusive, invasive, rude, and brutal.
But don't worry—this assignment is none of those things. Your aim is to produce a
portrait of a stranger that conveys intimacy, directness, and energy. You don't ask
for permission—you take your shot and move on.

This type of candid street portrait isn't as difficult or as daunting as it sounds. In fact,
once you get into it, this can be quite addictive. Practice your skills at an event such
as a protest. There will be hundreds of people with cameras and the protestors will
be used to being photographed. This is a great way to boost your confidence.

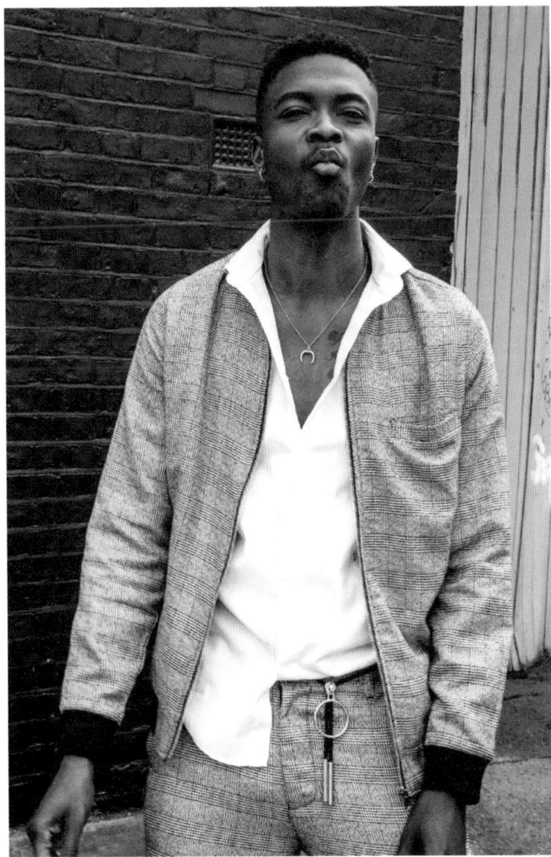

◄ If people look interesting, characterful, or cool, they're probably not bothered by the attention and won't bat an eyelid.

PRO TIP

Avoid eye contact with your subjects. Instead, look beyond them when you take the picture. In fact, avoid any kind of engagement—get your shot and carry on walking. If you're questioned about what you're doing, just smile, relax, and explain that you're working on a project. Try to avoid confrontation and delete a picture if it helps calm the situation.

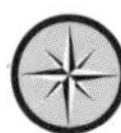
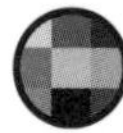

TECHNIQUE

- Be patient with your friend—they probably haven't done this before.

- Calming music can really help your model relax—a portable speaker and a suitable Spotify playlist are ideal for this.

- Chat to your friend while you're shooting to help them feel comfortable; people who aren't professional models can feel awkward, so you need to work a little harder to get them relaxed.

▶ *Use soft, natural light early or late in the day to flatter your model.*

THE PROCESS

Follow these steps to help make the experience a success:

1 Think about your goal for the shoot and choose your model accordingly. They don't need to have model "looks" or experience, just a willingness to get into the spirit of things.

2 Devise a plan and explain to your friend that you would like to practice your portrait skills. Make it clear that it's all very informal and that it will be a fun experience for both of you.

3 Think about the style of the portrait—formal, traditional, casual, contemporary, environmental, candid?

4 Create a mood board (maybe using Pinterest) and show your friend examples of the kind of portraits you would like to create.

5 Allow plenty of time for the shoot—if neither of you are very experienced it may take longer than you anticipate.

6 Discuss clothes and looks with your friend well in advance of the shoot and, if appropriate, suggest they bring a few different outfits. If they have an interesting or particularly glamorous outfit, encourage them to bring it along.

7 Always offer to provide your friend with a set of prints or digital files from the shoot as a thank you for their time.

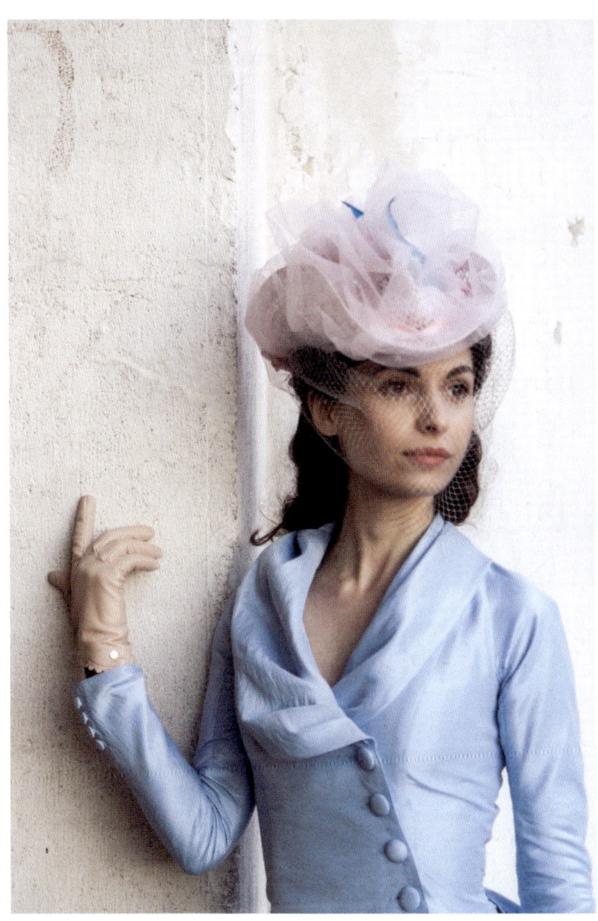

YOUR FRIEND, THE MODEL

Many of us would like to shoot a portrait using a model but it can be an expensive business. So, why not ask a friend to model for you? This is a fun assignment that will almost certainly be enjoyed by both parties. You can hire a studio, set up a light or two in your spare room, or—and this is the simplest option—find a suitable outdoor space for the shoot.

Don't start shooting without a plan or concept—think about the results you want to achieve and what "look" you're aiming for. Is it a moody portrait? A business portrait for a social media profile? A fashion vibe? Visualize the result and work out how you will achieve that in terms of the model's outfit, the lighting, poses, expressions, and props.

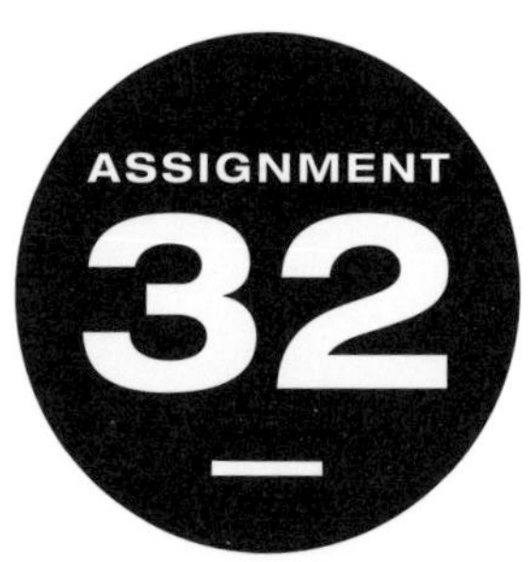

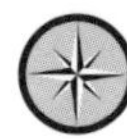

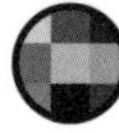

TECHNIQUE

- Find a good light source such as light from a shop window, neon sign, streetlamp, or even your subject's smartphone. Remember, this is all about making use of ambient light so leave your flash in the bag.

- Look for interesting colors of light and try to get some of these falling on your subject's face.

- Focus on the eyes and don't worry too much about what else is in focus.

- Think "dark and moody" rather than "bright and breezy"—night-time portraits are all about mood and atmosphere and you should aim for something dark and soulful.

- Always shoot in Raw so you can recover shadow detail later if necessary.

- Try the "fishing" technique adopted by street photographers: find a great light source and wait patiently for the subject to enter the scene.

- Be aware of your surroundings, particularly who's around you, and travel light—don't have all your expensive gear on show.

DARK IS THE NIGHT

If you've never shot an outdoor portrait at night using only ambient light, here's your chance. The city streets are aglow with lights of many different colors, temperatures, and intensities, so make the most of what's on offer. Embrace the endless creative possibilities!

This can be a posed portrait of someone you know or a shot of a stranger (if you're asking a stranger for a portrait, you'll find lot of tips in Assignment #9). The purpose of this assignment is to help you see the potential that's all around us on the streets at night; it's easy to dismiss this environment as being too dark when, in fact, it presents us with masses of opportunities.

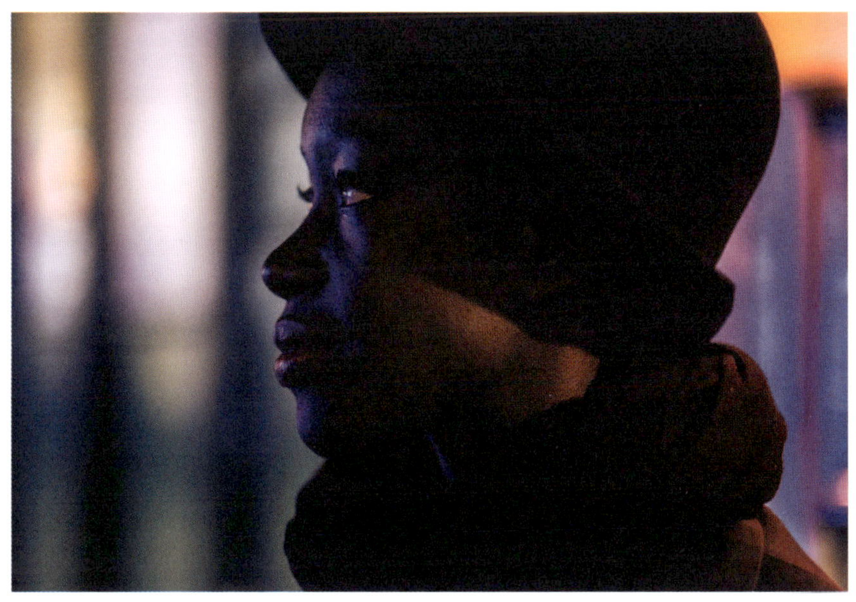

▲ *A little deliberate underexposure, using the exposure compensation dial, can help control the highlights and subdue any stray ambient light.*

ASSIGNMENT JOURNAL

PRO TIP

As a fast aperture is your prime consideration, shoot in aperture-priority mode with these settings:

- Select auto ISO with a ceiling of 6,400 (you'll need to get used to high ISO).

- Use the widest aperture possible— f/1.4 or f/1.8 is ideal and should give you a fast enough shutter speed to avoid camera shake.

- Use exposure compensation to fine-tune the exposure.

- As you'll have many different forms of artificial light to contend with, set your white balance to auto and deal with any adjustments in post-production.

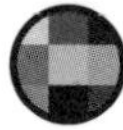

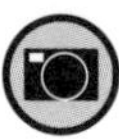

TECHNIQUE

- You can take readings from multiple positions to get an accurate average reading, perhaps from different parts of the face.

- The meter will only measure the light falling on your subject, so remember to take the background into consideration when setting your camera. A background that is significantly brighter or darker than your subject may affect the exposure of your portrait.

- Practice with your meter. It can feel like an unfamiliar and confusing tool at first, but you'll soon be using it intuitively.

PRO TIP

Before using your meter, there are two types of meter reading to be aware of: incident and reflected.

Incident metering is read from the subject's position and represents the amount of light falling on the subject (usually their face). As it doesn't consider the light reflecting off the subject, it's usually thought to be the most accurate method of metering for portraits—and this is what you should try for this assignment. A meter that takes incident readings usually has a white dome which gathers the light.

Reflected metering is taken from the photographer's position and measures the intensity of light "reflecting" off the subject or whole scene (this is typically what your camera's meter does).

THE PROCESS

Follow these six steps to use incident metering with flash:

1 Set your camera's ISO to its lowest setting—usually 100 or 200.

2 Set your shutter speed to your camera's highest sync speed, which is usually marked by a red flash symbol on the shutter speed dial, or you'll find it in your camera's manual.

3 Transfer these two settings to your light meter.

4 Make sure your meter "talks" to the camera, either using a sync cable or in "non-cord" mode.

5 Position the meter near your subject's chin and press the button on the meter to trigger the flash.

6 Read the aperture value from the meter for correct exposure and set your lens aperture to this.

LOVE YOUR METER

When most modern cameras have built-in exposure meters, do you really need an additional handheld meter to shoot portraits? While it's not essential, you'll find that with flash and mixed-lighting situations it's a very useful addition to your kit bag. One thing is for certain: it can help you produce more accurate results.

For this assignment, you'll become familiar with a meter and understand how it can help you take great portraits using flash. Metering in modern cameras is now so good that handheld meters are often overlooked, but they shouldn't be! By taking a reading with a meter, especially when using flash, you'll get an accurate exposure much more quickly and without the need to waste time experimenting with different settings.

You don't need a sophisticated or expensive model—there are plenty of secondhand examples around—but if you plan to use flash, make sure you get one with flash capability.

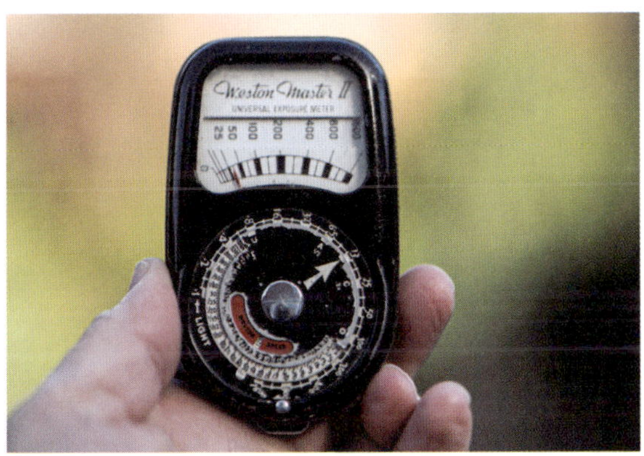

◀ *This old selenium meter is fine for ambient light—perfect for outdoor portraits or those with continuous lighting—but it's no use for flash in the studio.*

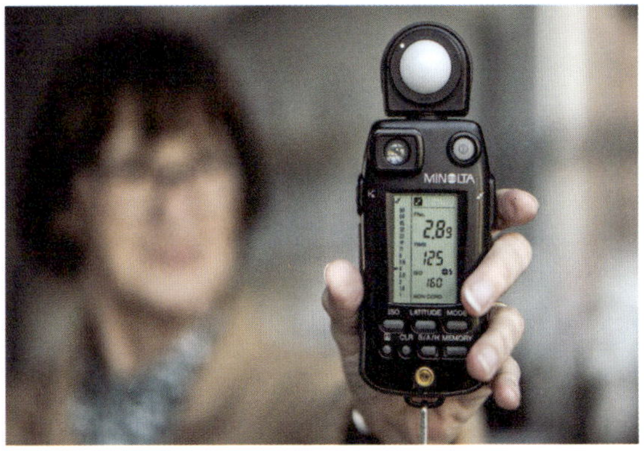

◀ *A more sophisticated meter should allow you to measure both flash and ambient light. Make sure your meter can take incident readings (if it has a white translucent dome like this one, it probably can).*

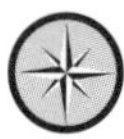

TECHNIQUE

- Think about the documentary possibilities of your portrait—"faceless" portraits can offer great storytelling potential. For example, a picture of someone walking away from the camera along a misty path could be the cover of a spy novel.

- Try standing back or zooming out to give your figure more space to "breathe" in the frame.

- Try introducing objects or props—a newspaper or book, the subject's hands, or a hat being held over the face—to obscure the face "by design."

PRO TIP

Shooting conceptual portraits such as this doesn't come easy to many photographers, as you need to throw convention to the wind and "unlearn" some of the rules of portraiture. Experiment and you'll be rewarded by trying ideas that might initially appear to be dumb.

▶ *You don't need to obscure all the face. In this example, around a quarter of the face is visible, helping create a sense of mystery.*

BACK TO BASICS

Portraits are not always about the whole of the face. Some would say that photographing someone from behind is likened to timidity or even voyeurism. However, "faceless" portraiture, which obscures some or all of your subject's face, gives the viewer more to think about; it creates a sense of intrigue, letting the viewer's mind fill in the gaps and create their own story about the subject.

This can be a posed portrait of someone you know or a candid one of a stranger. Without a face, you need to find something compelling to make the image sufficiently interesting; it could be an item of clothing, something about their outline, or perhaps the light. If the face is partly visible, try to keep the eyes obscured. Without the distraction of faces, eyes, and smiles, the background becomes more important so make sure it contributes something to the image.

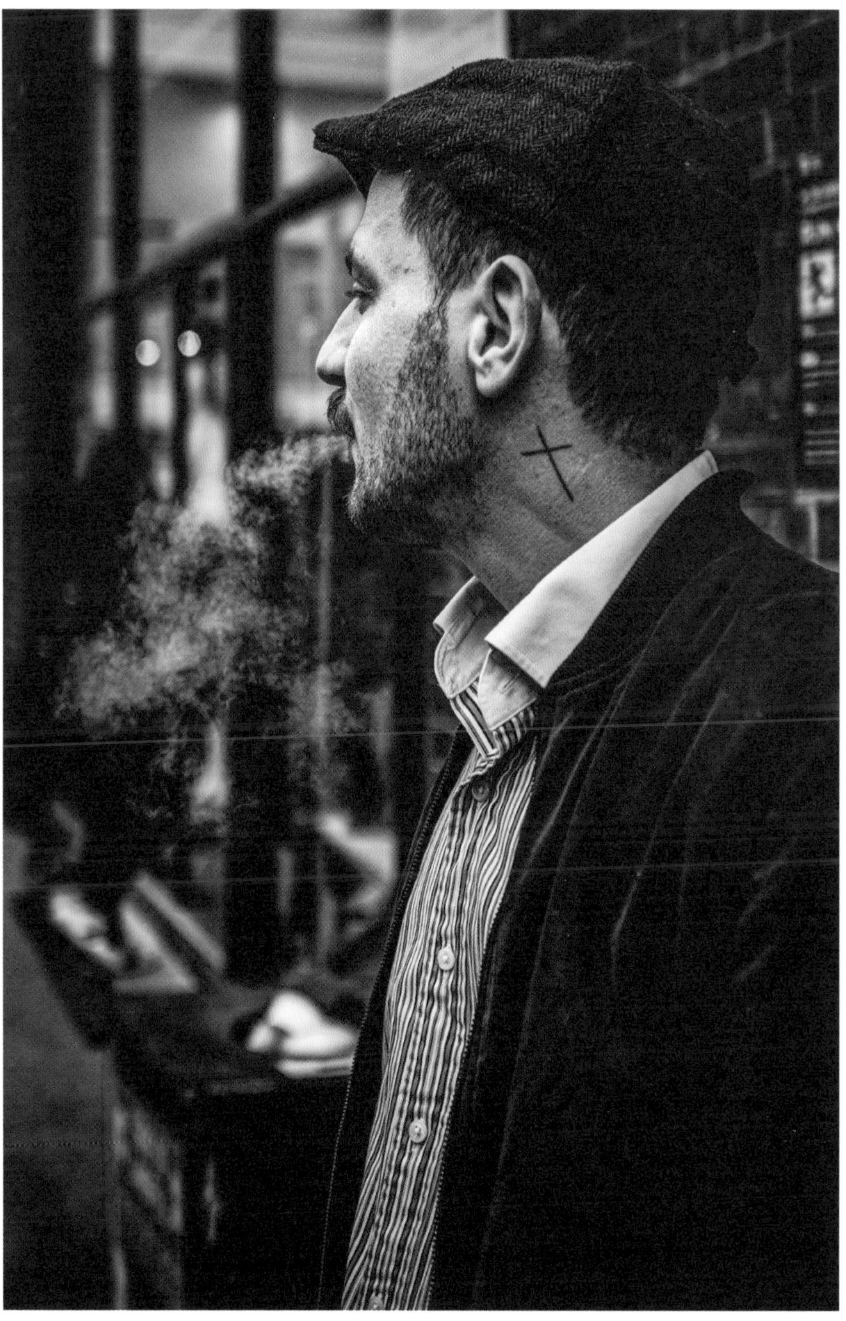

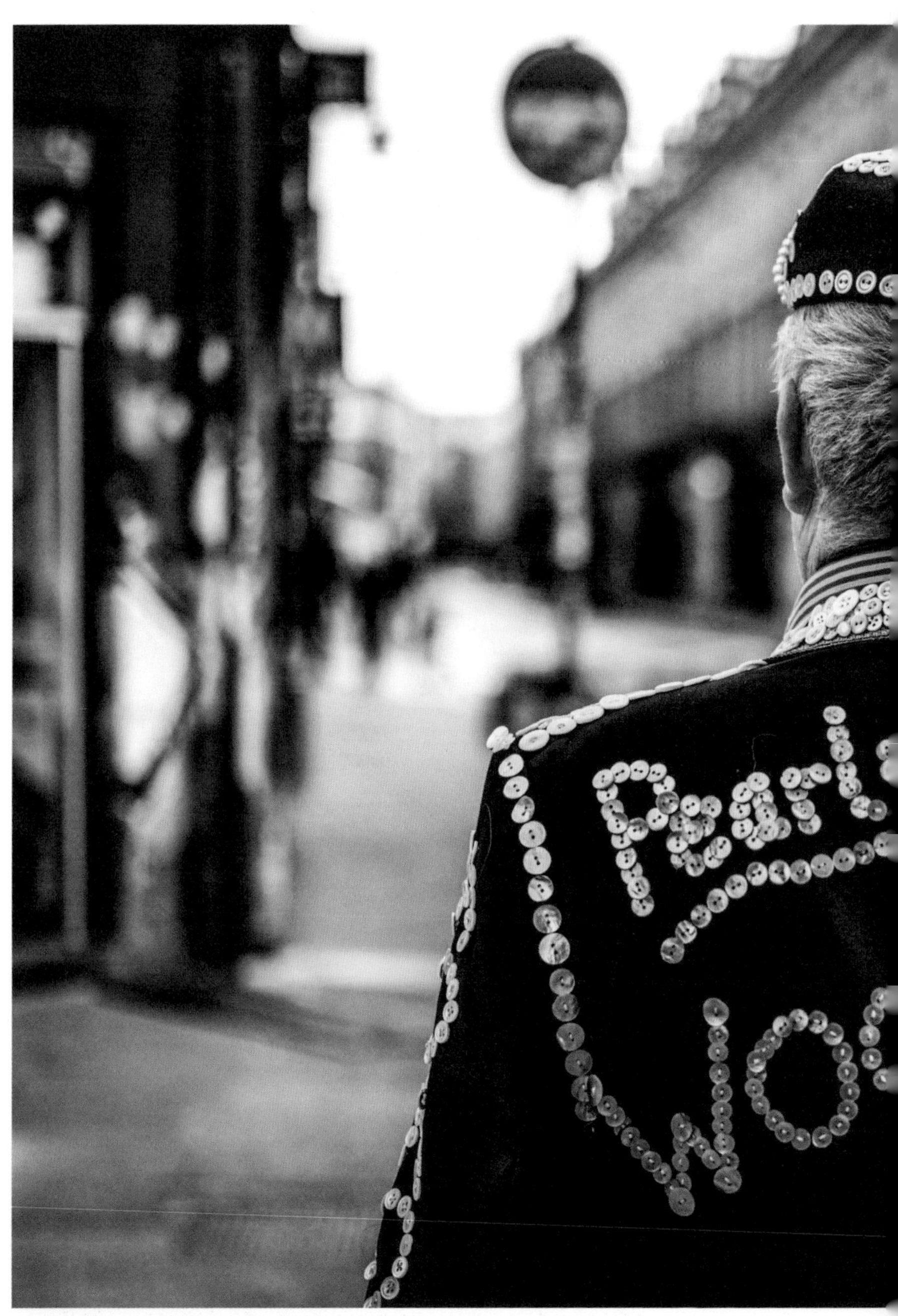

▲ *Arguably the most important information in this "faceless"
portrait is the information on the subject's back.*

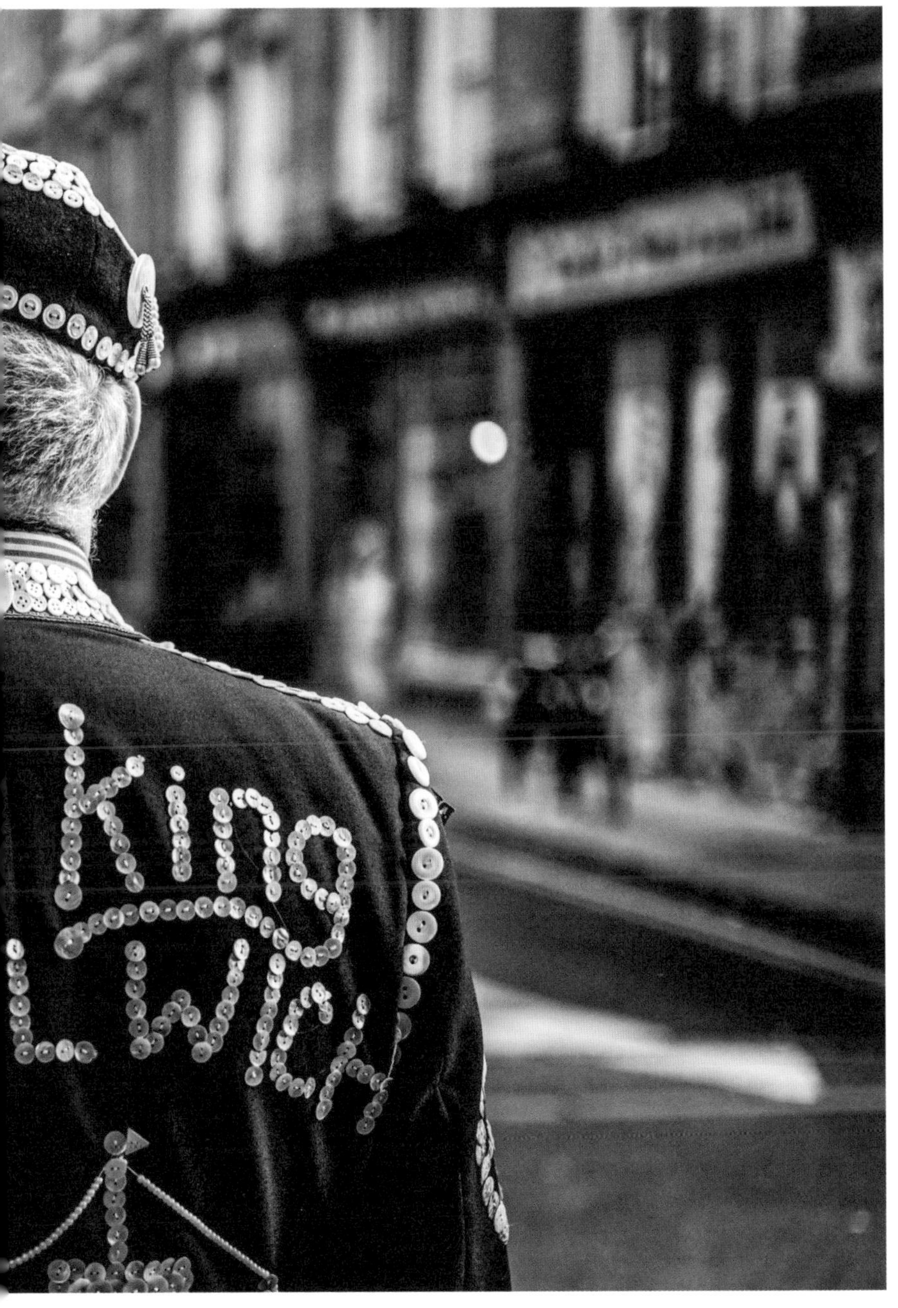
King
Wick

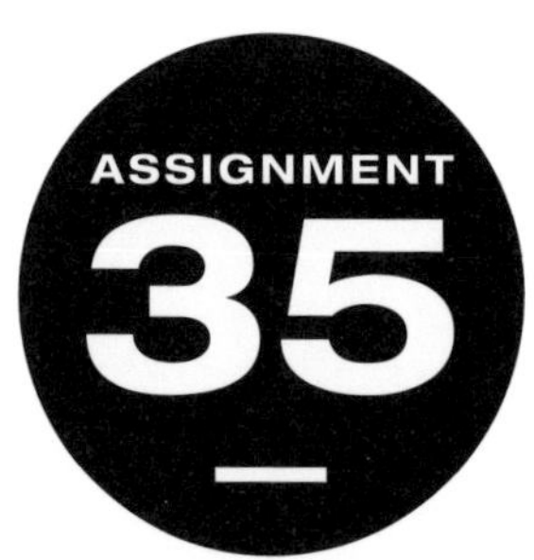

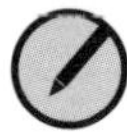

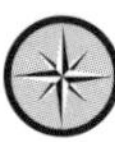

TECHNIQUE

- If you're not confident about your portrait-shooting abilities, practice on friends and family before the shooting starts for real.

- Don't worry about how "good" you think your photography is. Many organizations are grateful for whatever they can get and any images you provide can be put to good use on websites, social media etc.

- Although this is a learning exercise, treat it as a "professional" assignment as though you were being paid for the work.

- Have some business cards printed—one thing usually leads to another, and you'll probably be asked to get involved in other projects.

DO YOUR BIT

This is where documentary meets portrait photography. Why not put your portrait skills to good use and do your bit for the community? For this assignment, you'll need to find a charity or other local organization that could make use of some good photography. It's a great way to practice and develop your portrait photography skills while helping a good cause.

Find the right organization to approach and ask them if you can help them by taking some pictures that illustrate the work they do. Show them a few of your images and make it clear that no payment is expected. Have a plan before you make contact. Why are you doing this? Who will benefit? What will the pictures look like? How will they be used? Pre-empt all possible questions.

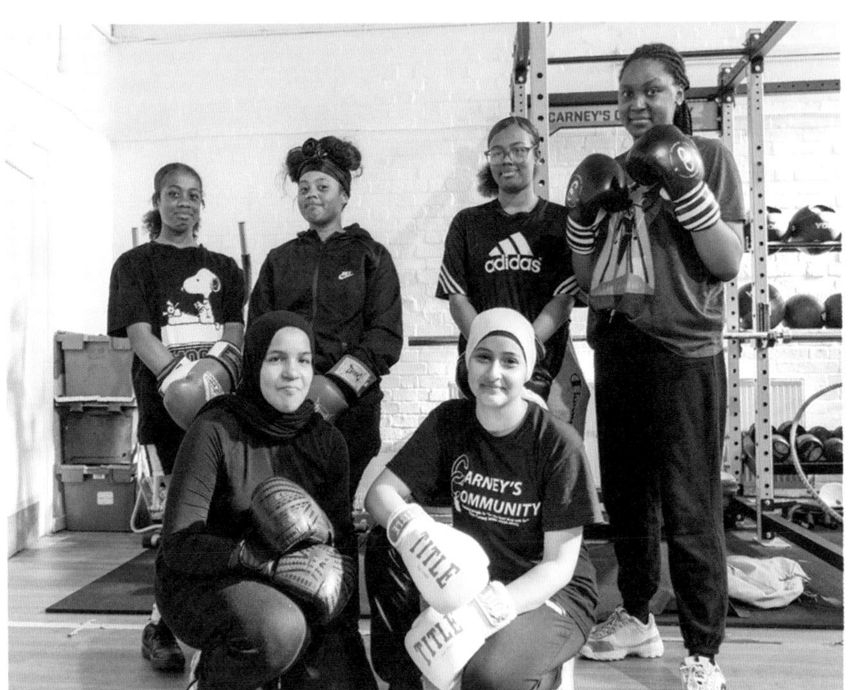

▲ Take the viewer on a journey with a wide range of pictures that includes establishing (wide) shots, close-up details, and, of course, portraits. Vary your portraits to include formal, informal, close-up, full-length, and action shots. Always take more images than you think you'll need.

PRO TIP

The best way to describe how to go about this assignment is to examine a real-world example and we're going to look at an ongoing project by London photographer Nick Cornwall. Nick approached Carney's Community, a charity-based boxing gym, and asked if he could document the work they do in getting disadvantaged young people off the street by giving them skills, discipline, and self-respect, using boxing as the medium. To attract funding via donations, it's important for Carney's to send out a strong message about the good they do, and what better way to do this than by using photography? So, after several years of shooting life in the gym, Nick has produced a great set of images— for inspiration, visit www.carneyscommunity.org.

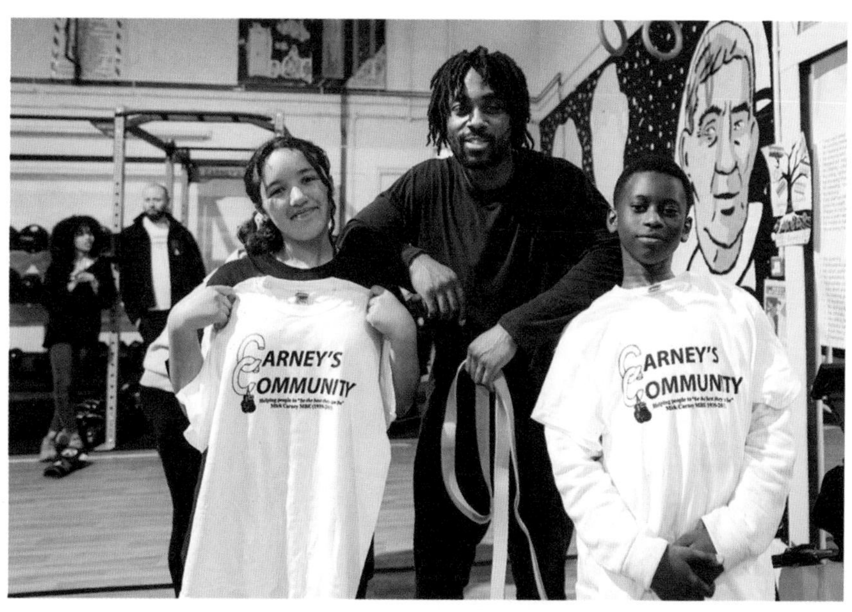
CARNEY'S
COMMUNITY
CARNEY'S
COMMUNITY

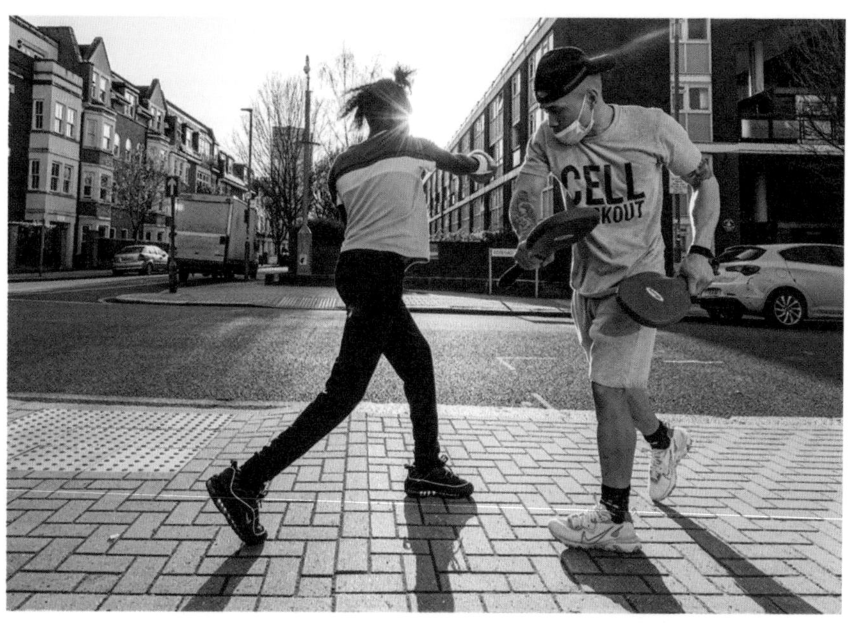
CELL
WORKOUT

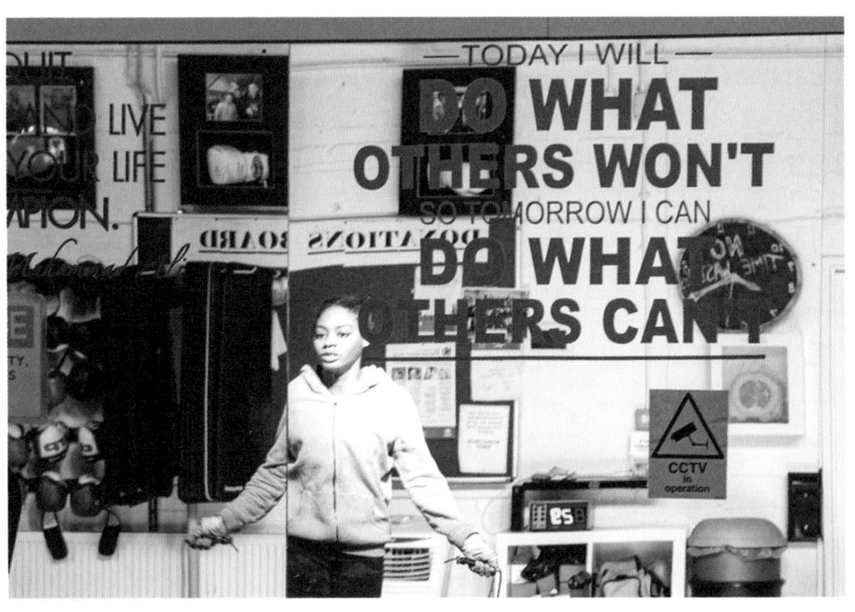

ASSIGNMENT JOURNAL

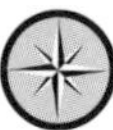

TECHNIQUE

- Take a variety of shots—some wide showing the context, some from the middle distance, and some close-up showing the detail.

- You'll probably need to guide your subject in terms of their expression. Ideally, you want to show them to be content, proud, or satisfied, surrounded by their possessions.

- You can do this using flash, continuous, or natural lighting. If using artificial light, beware of unwanted shadows—you want balanced, even lighting.

- Your "money shot" will probably show the collector surrounded by their objects, all in sharp focus, but do experiment with depth of field. Try some shots with everything in focus, some with just the person in focus, and some where the focus is on the objects.

- Consider creating a more abstract portrait. For example, if your subject's passion is making their own clothes, drape a strip of colorful fabric across their face.

PRO TIP

These images were all shot using a mixture of natural light (through two skylights) and a fluorescent tube. With mixed lighting like this, take care to find a white balance setting that gives a natural-looking result.

GET PASSIONATE

Many of us get very passionate about our possessions and this assignment is all about creating a portrait of someone for whom the objects of their desire form a big part of their lives—collectors, for example.

Your challenge in this assignment is to find someone who's surrounded by interesting objects such as a stamp collector, someone with a wine cellar, a collector of porcelain, or a grower of bonsai trees. You'll be shooting a portrait that gives equal importance to the person and their possessions, and which shows a connection between them.

A portrait of a collector should capture the passion and dedication (and sometimes obsession) they bring to their collecting, as well as the unique beauty and value of the items they have gathered over time.

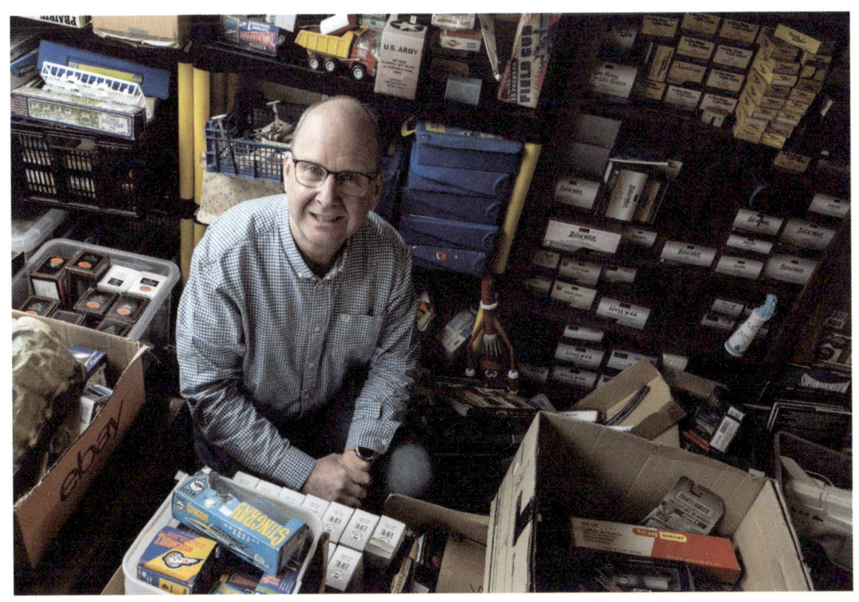

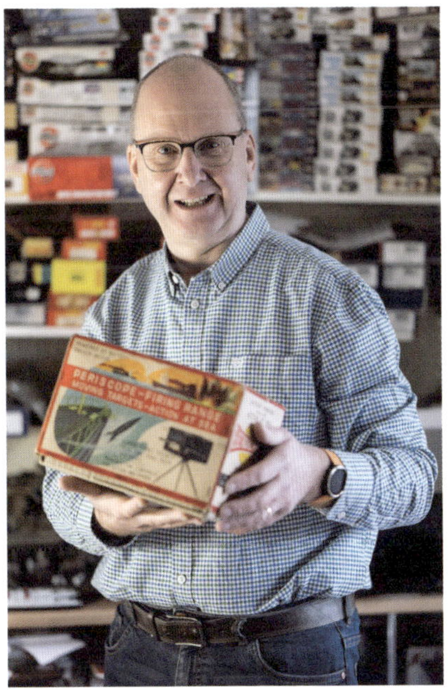

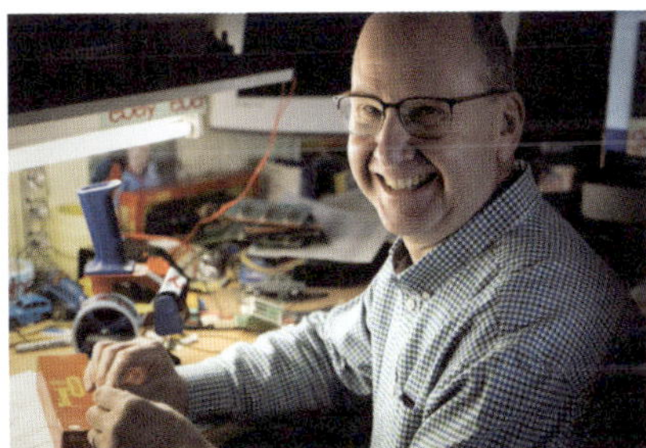

◀ *These images show a collector of models—toy cars, boats, airplanes, trains, and figures. He buys them, repairs them, cleans them, and sometimes sells them. His workroom is a chaotic mass of models, boxes, and tools, and the pictures were taken to reflect some of that chaos rather than shooting him in a bland, sanitized environment.*

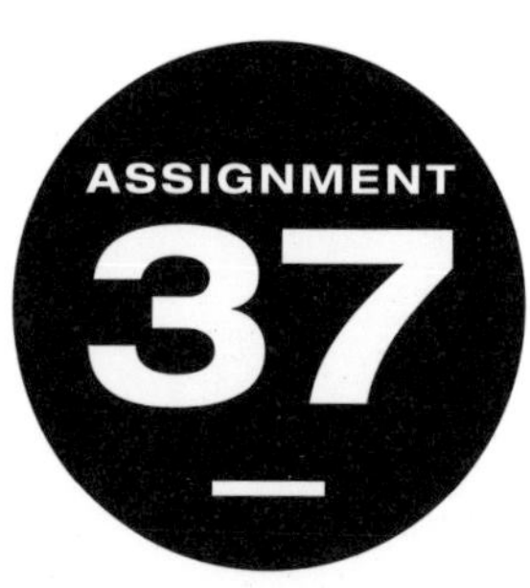

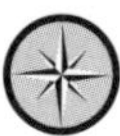

TECHNIQUE

- Make the background as important as the artist. A wider shot incorporating the artist's habitat can tell you a lot about them and their working life—just watch out for distracting clutter that diverts the eye.

- Use natural light wherever possible and keep an eye on your white balance.

- Use a tripod, select a small aperture to keep the background sharp, and opt for a low ISO to maximize image quality.

- Artists are often unconventional people, so don't feel constrained by "norms" and experiment with perspectives, angles, and lighting techniques.

ASSIGNMENT JOURNAL

PRO TIP

Artists can sometimes be introverts—the most creative people often are—so you may need to exercise your people skills to get the best out of them. Get them chatting about their art, their training, and their business, as it will help them relax into the shoot. Always offer to send them a few images from the shoot—artists are always in need of good portraits for self-promotion and, if they like your work, they'll probably spread the word about you.

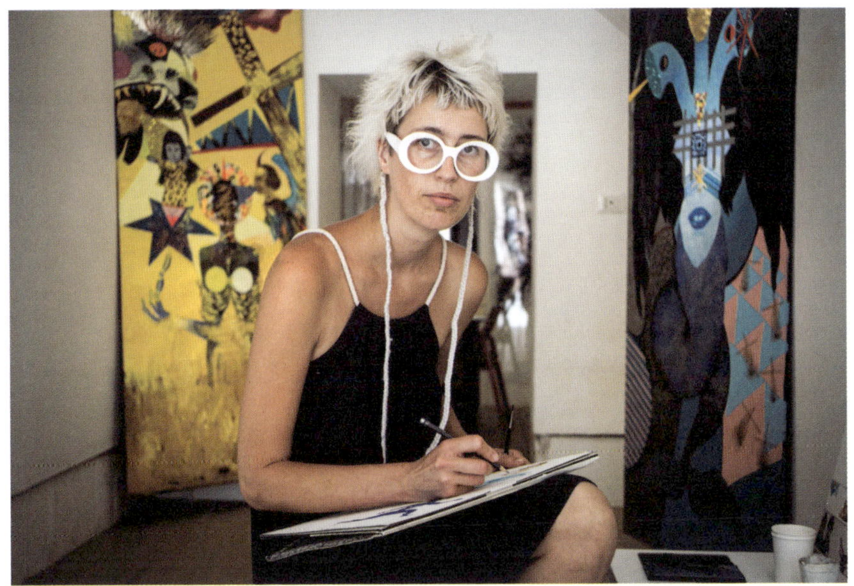

PORTRAIT OF AN ARTIST

Artists and their studios can make wonderful subjects for portraits. They generally look interesting and tend to inhabit colorful spaces. For this assignment, you should find a local artist—painter, sculptor, or even photographer—and ask them if you can take their portrait in their studio.

This assignment is designed to make you think about the space your subject inhabits and how they relate to it. It should be well lit and detailed, though not too distracting, and showing some of the artist's work. It's a fine balance between including the detail and ensuring it doesn't overpower the subject—your attention to detail is critical here.

This would be the ideal assignment to lead you into a bigger project. Artists often know other artists and are part of formal or informal networks. So, once you've done a good job with one artist you should be able to use that as a calling card to speak to others, which could lead to a great body of work at least worthy of a zine or book.

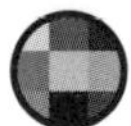

TECHNIQUE

- Shoot in Raw for total control over the tonal range and use the Contrast, Blacks, and Whites sliders to achieve deep blacks and bright whites (while taking care not to blow out the highlights).

- Select your camera's monochrome mode—this will allow you to review images in black and white while you shoot, and convert and edit your images later, giving you more creative options.

- Look for a simple background that isn't too distracting—you're aiming for a minimalist look with this assignment.

- Keep an eye on your histogram—your whites should be bright but be careful not to blow them out. Conversely, don't be afraid to keep the shadow areas very dark.

- Careful dodging and burning in post-production will allow you to emphasize contrast in specific areas of the frame.

MONO MAGIC

When we shoot in color, we have the luxury of achieving contrast with variations in hue, saturation, and luminance. With black and white, we have only tone to work with, but by using big variations in tone, we can create striking, evocative, and contrasty portraits. When we look at black-and-white portraits, we tend to experience a wider gamut of feelings than we would with color: soulfulness, nostalgia, or artistry, for example.

This assignment is all about contrast: you'll be aiming for deep, inky blacks and crisp, bright whites. You can use any model, but you'll find it easier if there is some natural contrast in their appearance, for example pale skin and dark hair or dark skin and light clothing. This look will be best achieved indoors and needs only minimum kit—a one-light setup is ideal, or you can use just natural light from a window.

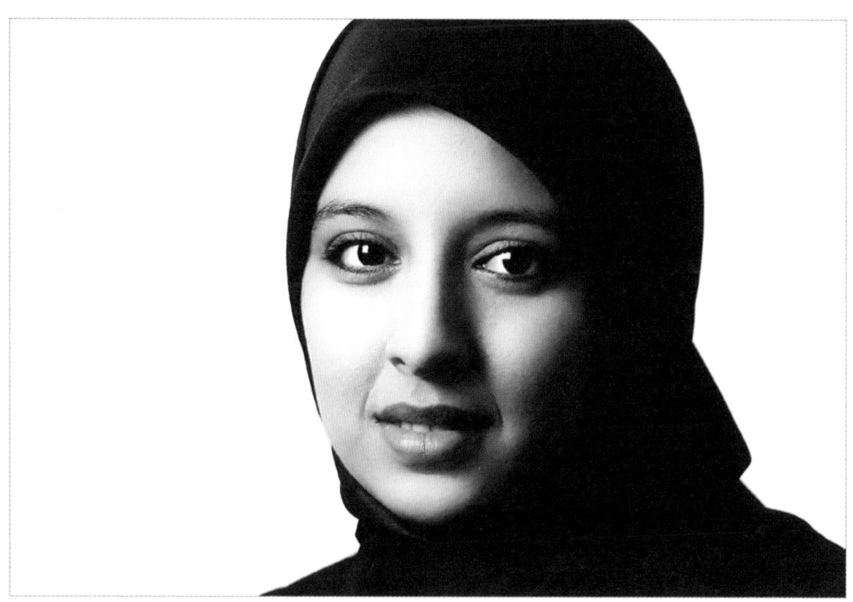

▲ *This black-and-white portrait was shot with a one-light setup using a large softbox to the left of the camera.*

PRO TIP

With a contrasty portrait, the harsh light can be unflattering, so take the edge off this harshness by using soft light modifiers such as a softbox. Remember that the bigger the softbox, the softer the light, and the closer the softbox is to the subject, the softer the light.

ASSIGNMENT JOURNAL

TECHNIQUE

- Avoid interlocking fingers and try not to have either the back of hands or the palms facing the camera.

- Direct your subject's hand pose and ask them to bend their knuckles and fingers slightly, conveying relaxed body language.

- Take care to pose the hands to avoid the "missing finger" illusion, when one finger eclipses another.

- If you're using artificial light, pose your subject's hands so they're not catching the light full on, as this could make them overly bright and distracting.

- Shoot with a focal length of 50mm or longer—if you use a wide lens, the hands will look out of proportion to the face.

- If your subject is active, use as fast a shutter speed as possible, as you need the hands to be sharp. Aim for 1/125 sec. or faster.

PRO TIP

Make sure hands aren't tightly clasped, as this can look stressful, particularly the "white knuckle" look, and never crop across wrists, hands, or fingers, as this can make the image feel incomplete.

HANDY WORK

Giving the hands a useful role can help make your subject feel less awkward and create a more balanced, natural portrait. After all, "What shall I do with my hands?" is probably the most-asked question during portrait shoots and the "hand pose" is an important element of the shot. So, in this assignment, you'll help your subject along by directing them a little and suggesting they do something specific with their hand(s). Here are a few ideas:

- Hands in pockets or on hips for a casual look.
- Hold an object such as a bunch of flowers.
- Engage in an activity, such as writing, raising a glass toward the mouth, or running fingers through the hair.
- Touch the clothing—holding the lapels is a classic pose.
- Use gestures to add expression or perhaps to frame the face.
- Arms raised—hands clasped behind the head can be a great look.

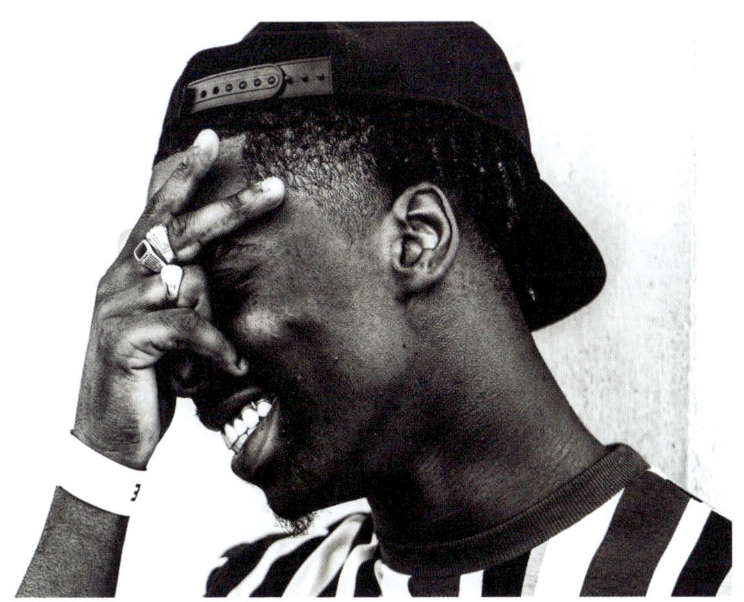

▲ *Use gestures to add emotion and drama to a portrait.*

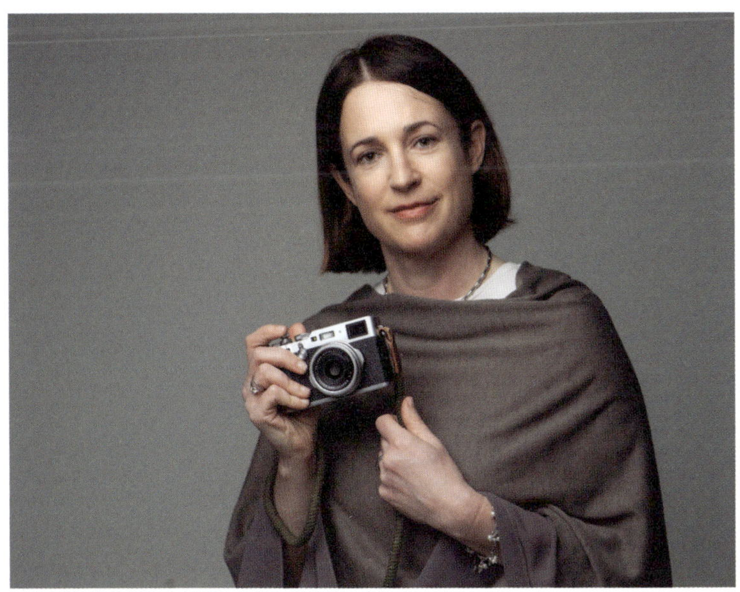

▲ *A relevant prop can add context as well as giving the hands a useful role.*

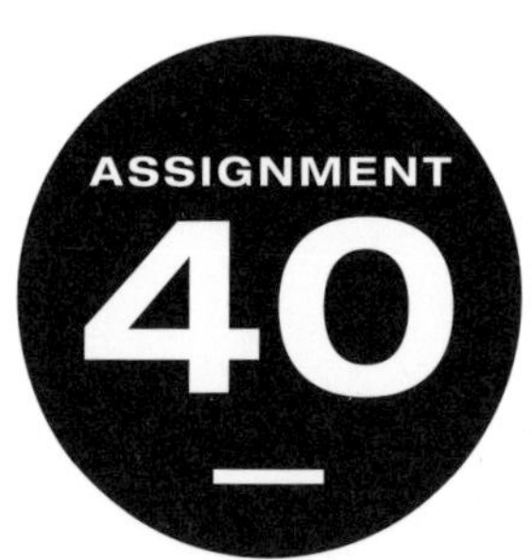

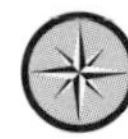

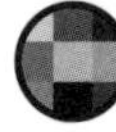

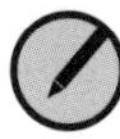

TECHNIQUE

- Use natural light. Avoid the middle of the day when the light is harsh and make the most of cool blue mornings or warm golden afternoons or evenings.

- Choose your background carefully—it should complement the subject and be "outdoorsy," whether rural or urban, but not overly cluttered.

- Decide whether you need the background to be in or out of focus and select the aperture accordingly—try to pre-visualize the result before you pick up your camera.

- Avoid erroneous intrusions into your shot such as telegraph poles or power lines.

- Select single-point AF mode and position the AF point over the subject's face for precision focusing.

THE GREAT OUTDOORS

For this assignment, you'll be shooting an outdoor portrait that conveys space, freedom, and openness. Shooting in natural light, you should aim to incorporate attractive elements such as trees, open landscapes, or photogenic buildings.

Shooting outdoor portraits can be more challenging than shooting indoors, as you have no control over the weather or lighting conditions. You need to think carefully about the direction and quality of the light and how the background will benefit (or detract from) the portrait. It's a good idea to plan the location in advance, ideally doing a recce visit before the shoot and thinking about the direction of the light, the background, and whether you need any permission to shoot there.

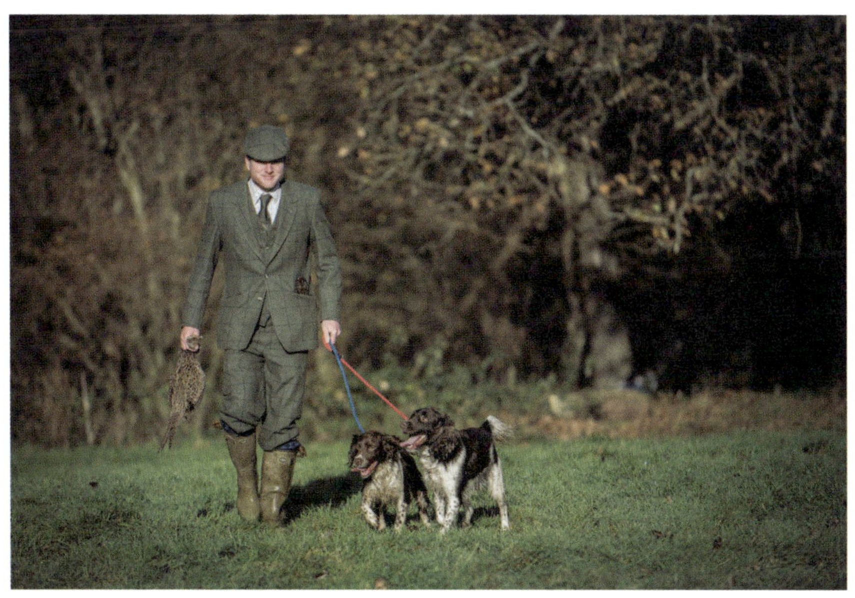

▲ *Outdoor portraits don't always have to be closely cropped—sometimes a wider context suits the shot better.*

ASSIGNMENT JOURNAL

____

____

____

____

____

____

____

PRO TIP

A white or gold reflector may be useful to bounce light into any shadow areas on your subject's face. In cloudy conditions, a gold reflector will add warmth to the skin tones. In warm light, a white reflector will give a more natural look. If you don't have an "assistant" to hold the reflector for you, it could be hung from a lighting stand or tripod, or even from the branch of a tree.

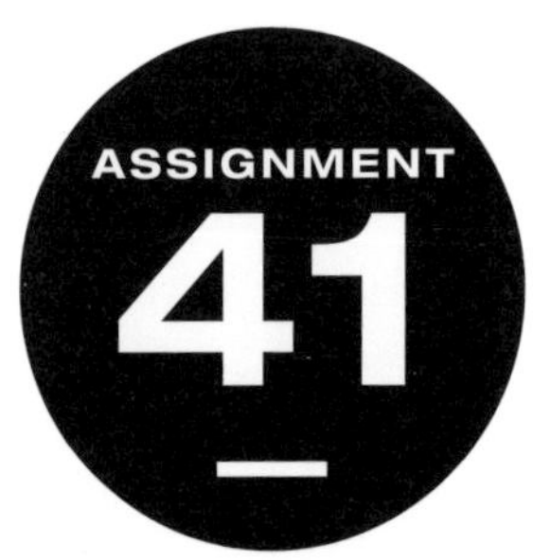

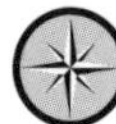

TECHNIQUE

- Try to link the subject to the story (in the way that a man in a gray suit standing outside an office wouldn't). Consider, for example, incorporating elements that are important to the story: a prop, a specific location, an event taking place in the background.

- Position your subject in the best light, find a suitable background, and direct their pose and expression to fit your take on the story. The expression is crucial and should be appropriate for the tone of the article and the subject matter.

- A good rule in photojournalism is "less is more" so aim for a simple, clear portrait that conveys the message in an instant.

- Why stop here? You could use your portrait as the feature image for a wider photo-essay on your chosen news story.

HEADLINE ACT

Photojournalism is all about telling a story through photography and its role is to illustrate the news, dramatically but truthfully, in an insightful and visually compelling way. Newspapers and magazines are full of powerful images of news events but it's the photographs featuring people's faces that really grab our attention, as we are naturally drawn to people's eyes and they're usually the first thing we look at.

Your aim here is to shoot a portrait inspired by a current news story. This is a conceptual portrait in the sense that you find your story and "design" your image to fit. Look at what's happening in the news—it could be a local news story covered by your town's newspaper—and find someone involved in that story who could make a good portrait subject. The story could be political, social, or human interest, and it doesn't need to be a big story, just an important one.

Approaching a potential subject shouldn't be too difficult, as people are generally hungry for publicity for their story. Once you have a name, do a little research and approach them by email or social media and explain that you're working on a portrait project and would love to take their picture.

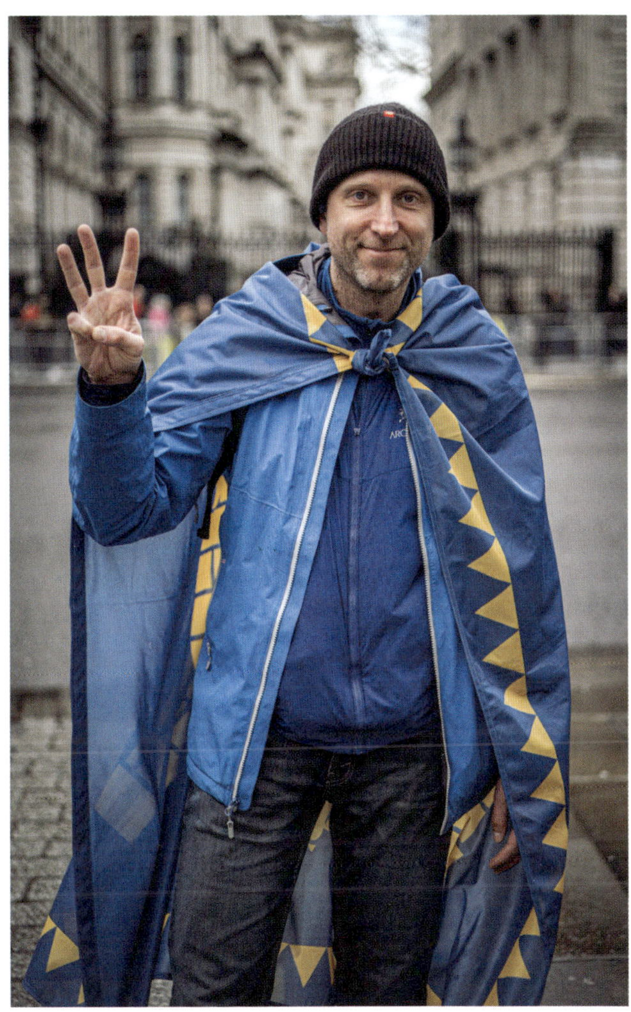

PRO TIP

Make sure you embed your name and contact details into the metadata of the image (you can easily do this in most post-production apps). Offer your subject the image to use for their own purposes but make it clear that if anyone else wants to use it, they must speak to you first. At the very least, you want a byline or photo credit, and you may even get a small fee.

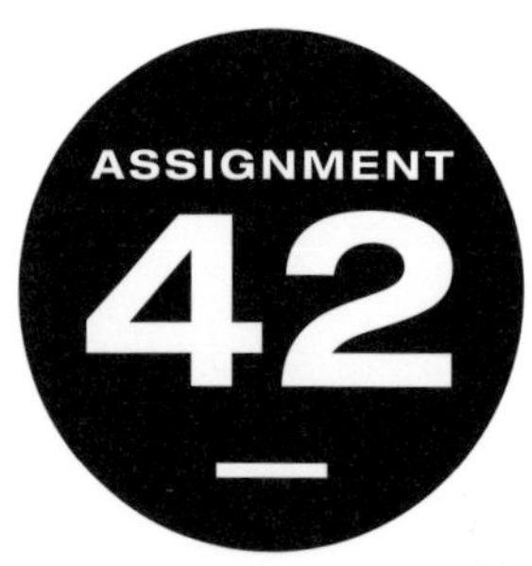

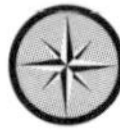

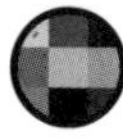

ASSIGNMENT JOURNAL

TECHNIQUE

- Frame tightly and focus on the eyes—a focal length of 50mm will help you forge an intimate connection with your subject.

- Ask your subject to choose an outfit that reflects their style and personality. This could be dapper, glamorous, arty, or punky.

- Choose either natural or artificial lighting. It's easier to create drama using flash, as you have greater control. On the other hand, daylight could create a softer, more sympathetic look. Don't be afraid to use very dramatic lighting such as the low-key effect (see Assignment #52).

- Encourage your subject to show their emotions and personality through their facial expressions and body language. You're aiming for authenticity, with body language that's in sync with the true character; pensive, relaxed, confident, intelligent, funny, eccentric . . . whatever works for that person.

PRO TIP

Don't be tempted to flatter with a character portrait. If your subject has wrinkles or scars, show them. If they have tattoos, emphasize them. It's all part of their character.

▶ *This character is a sailor, and the outfit was carefully chosen to reflect his personal style.*

CHARACTER STUDY

Shooting a character study is all about capturing an individual's personality, emotions, and individuality. Whereas conventional portraits usually aim to flatter, character portraits aim to tell a story, helping the viewer "understand" the subject, and go beyond mere superficial looks by probing more deeply into the subject's feelings, their state of mind, and even their inadequacies. These portraits usually aim to inform rather than beautify.

Your assignment is to create a simple, authentic, and honest character study of someone you know: a work colleague, friend, or neighbor. If you're stuck for ideas, think of the people you know who do interesting things—this is a good starting point.

Before you start shooting, take some time to interact with your subject, and establish a connection. Talk to them, ask questions, listen to their stories, and make them feel comfortable and at ease. This will help you capture their personality and emotions.

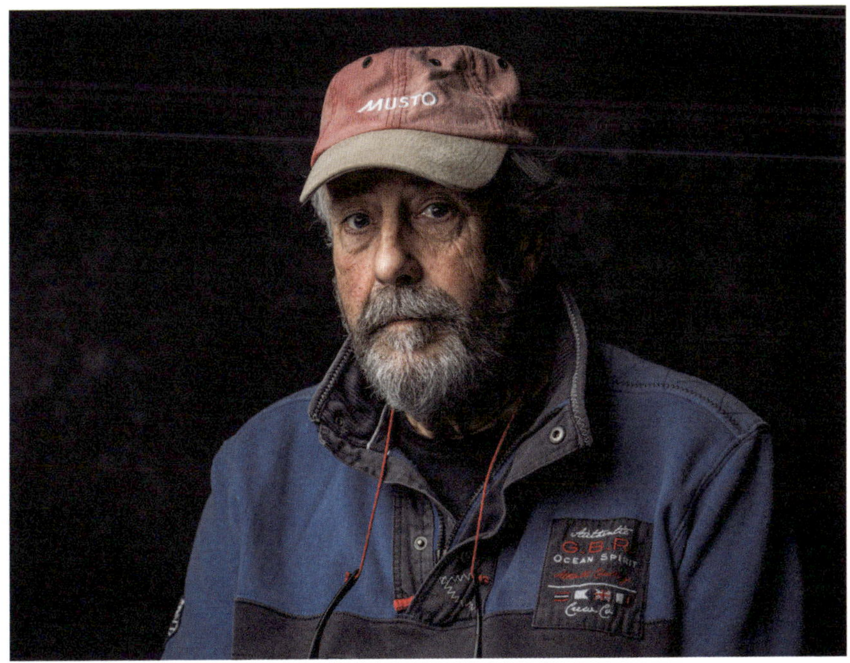

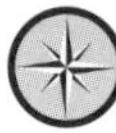

ASSIGNMENT JOURNAL

TECHNIQUE

- Practice your art until you're confident you can charge for your services. You don't need to be David Bailey, but you must be able to take a sharp, well-lit, perfectly exposed, and nicely posed portrait.

- Specialize. Stick with portraits initially and if you later branch out, expand into something complementary such as weddings or other forms of social photography. Don't mix your offering with, say, landscape or wildlife photography.

- Build a portfolio—ideally a website—and include the type of work you intend to sell. Show only your best images—less is more.

- Offer a wide variety of portrait shoots: babies, children, couples, individuals, family groups, graduates, business headshots, social media profile pictures, etc. You'll find it's a big market.

- Don't overinvest in gear. Many people make this mistake and find that they are funding the business rather than the business funding them. Buy only essential gear and consider hiring more expensive items, such as specialist lenses, when you need them for a specific project.

PRO TIP

Giving up the day job too quickly can be a mistake, as ambition doesn't pay the bills. Wait until you have a sustainable business before you take the plunge. It takes time to build a portfolio and business, so take small steps and don't expect too much at first.

MAKE IT PAY

If you enjoy shooting portraits, why not make some money from your hobby? Who knows, it may turn into something much bigger—lots of well-known portrait photographers including Cecil Beaton, David Bailey, and Rankin started in a very small way. There's always strong demand for good portrait photography and making money in this way is a perfectly reasonable aspiration.

While you need to have a certain level of skill and competence, you don't need to be a professional—you just need a professional approach. Don't be too ambitious at first. Outdoor portraits are very popular and you don't need lots of lighting gear to do a great job. Alternatively, buy some inexpensive flash gear and offer to shoot in people's homes. Whichever approach you take, so long as you're confident with your setup and approach, you'll find that word will get around and commissions will roll in.

Once you know you can take a good portrait and you're ready to give this a try, tell everyone—family, friends, and colleagues—that you're trying to earn money from your portrait photography. Spread the word—this isn't the time to be shy.

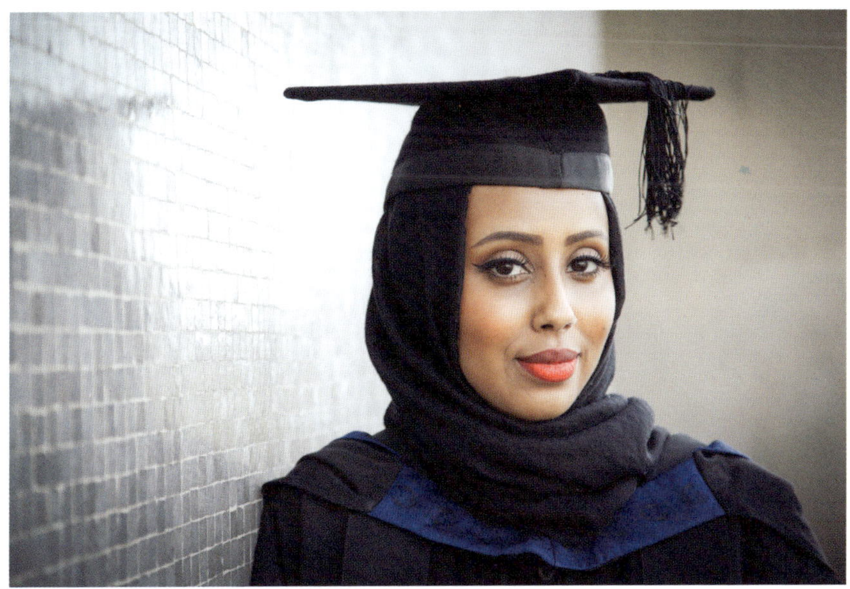

▲ *Consider shooting portraits at events such as graduation ceremonies, business functions, and social events. These are generally not too "technical" and can help build a portfolio.*

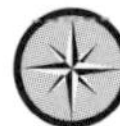

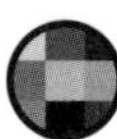

TECHNIQUE

- Aim for soft, natural, sympathetic lighting—covered shade is ideal if shooting outdoors.

- Encourage the couple to pose in a way that feels natural and comfortable—don't force them into anything too awkward or contrived. Emphasize their closeness with intimate poses, such as having their heads together, and ask them to interact and show genuine intimacy and emotion.

- Shoot a wide range of compositions from close-ups to much wider shots that highlight the importance of the location.

- Constantly communicate with the couple as you shoot to make them feel at ease.

- Be patient, don't rush things, and be ready to capture spontaneous moments of genuine emotion and affection.

LOVE IS THE DRUG

For this assignment, you'll be photographing a couple, whether they're engaged, married, or just good friends. This portrait is all about the connection between your subjects and the challenge is to make that apparent in your image.

To capture an authentic bond between two people, it's better to shoot a couple who have a genuine connection to each other rather than using models. Choose an attractive location that resonates with the couple in some way. This could be indoors, but an outside location usually works best—maybe a beach, park, countryside, or even a city backdrop—as this will give you the opportunity to use soft and natural, even romantic, lighting. Shoot around the golden hour, the hour after sunrise or before sunset, for soft light and a lovely warm glow.

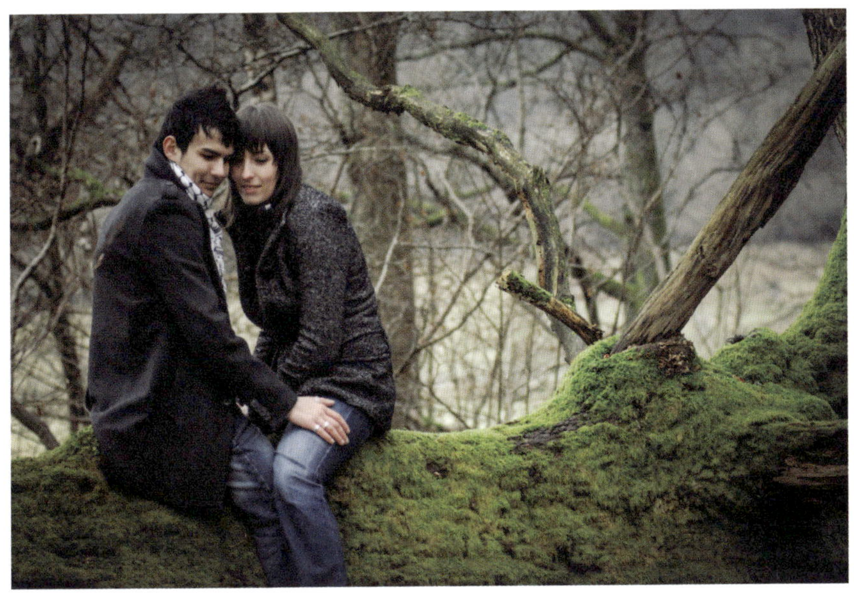

▲ *Your subjects don't necessarily need to look at the camera, or even into each other's eyes—just looking down can help convey the tender moment you're looking for.*

ASSIGNMENT JOURNAL

PRO TIP

Emphasize the dreaminess in post-production by adding a "glow" effect. Create an adjustment layer and duplicate it several times, adding different levels and intensities of Gaussian blur. You can also experiment with the blending modes to enhance the glow.

Alternatively, use a diffusion filter to create a soft in-camera effect. This will make the highlights bleed into the shadows, giving it a softened look.

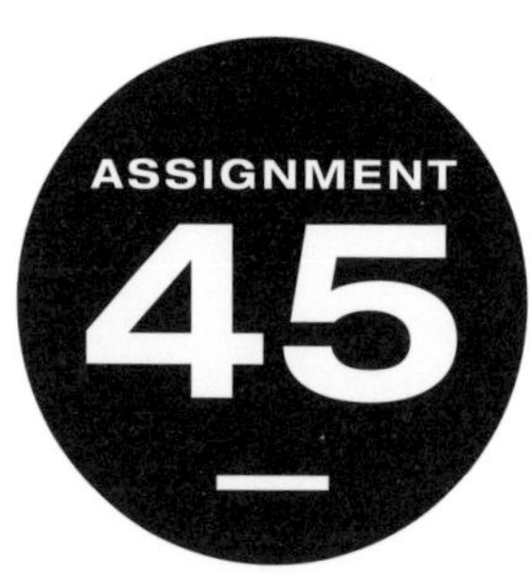

TECHNIQUE

- Find a willing subject. Some people will feel awkward being shot at odd angles, and if your model feels awkward, the image will look awkward.

- A tilted head or horizon can add tension, dynamism, and drama. Even small adjustments can bring an otherwise ordinary portrait to life.

- Have your subject lie down and shoot from directly overhead for a bird's-eye view.

- The Dutch angle can be used to create a sense of fun and liveliness, or alternatively feelings of disorientation, unease, or tension. The degree of tilt can vary, from slight to severe, usually between 5–90°.

- Make the most of your model's physical attributes. For example, shoot someone with a large chin from a higher angle or a person with a bald head from a lower angle.

▶ *Test the water with your model and see if they have a sense of fun. If so, this is your green light to throw convention to the wind.*

GOING DUTCH

In this assignment, you'll be using the Dutch angle to create a dynamic portrait. The Dutch angle (also referred to as the Dutch tilt, the oblique angle, or the canted angle) creates an unusual perspective by tilting the camera to create a portrait that forces the viewer to think—and look—twice.

In landscape photography, straight horizons and carefully proportioned elements are incredibly important. In portrait photography, convention isn't quite so prescribed, which means we can free ourselves from the "rules" and experiment to our heart's content, which is exactly what we're going to do here.

ASSIGNMENT JOURNAL

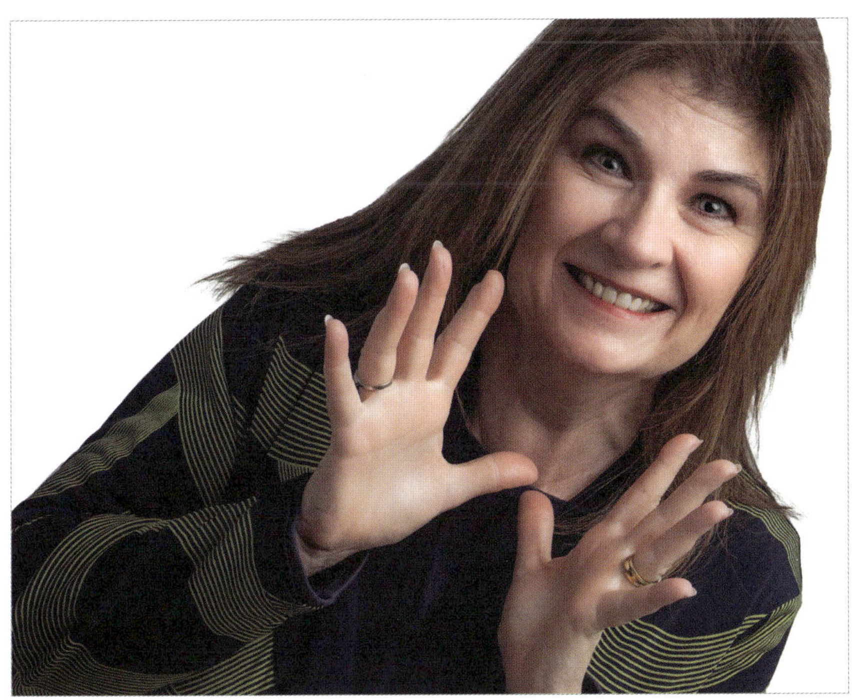

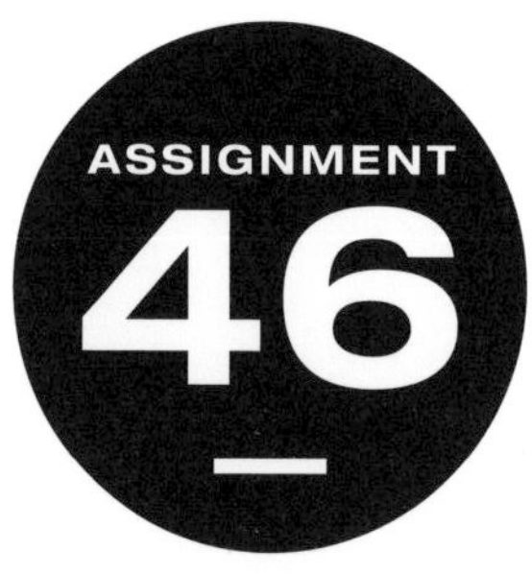

ASSIGNMENT 46

PRO TIP

If your bokeh contains small light sources such as car headlights or fairy lights, be careful to compose so that they are clear of the subject's head—you'll have a more pleasing portrait if the head is clear of distracting artefacts.

TECHNIQUE

- A lens with an aperture of f/2.8 or faster will create the most pronounced bokeh effect.

- A focal length between 50mm and 135mm will be perfect for your bokeh portrait. The longer the lens, the more the blur.

- Experiment with different apertures, starting at f/2.8. The wider the aperture, the shallower the depth of field and the stronger the bokeh effect.

- Ensure there's plenty of distance between subject and background—the greater the distance, the more bokeh you'll get.

- Find a background with plenty of small reflections or light sources.

▶ *Circular artefacts, particularly from distant lights, can create pleasing bokeh in portraits.*

ASSIGNMENT JOURNAL

BOKEH-LICIOUS

The term "bokeh" comes from the Japanese word "boke," which means blur or haze, resulting in "boke-aji," the "blur quality." But bokeh is different from simple blur in that it usually refers to the soft areas around small background highlights, resulting in a visually pleasing out-of-focus effect.

Your aim here is to shoot a portrait that makes bokeh a feature of the image, an effect achieved deliberately rather than a lucky by-product.

When shooting this assignment, it's worth bearing in mind that the background is just as important as the subject and it must have the right qualities to make the most of the bokeh opportunity. Look for background elements such as colorful leaves or bright lights that will complement your subject.

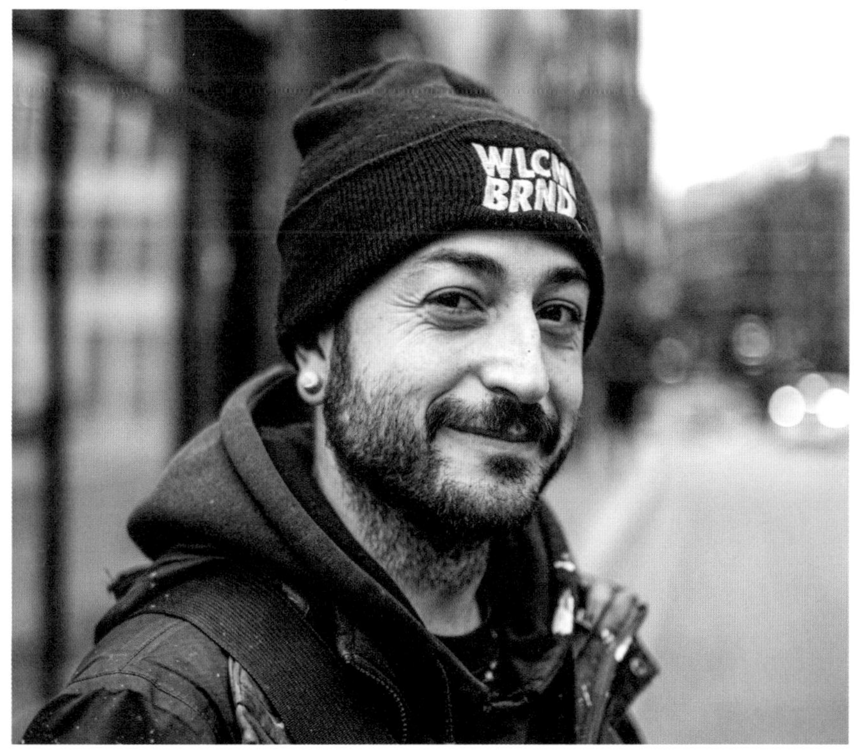

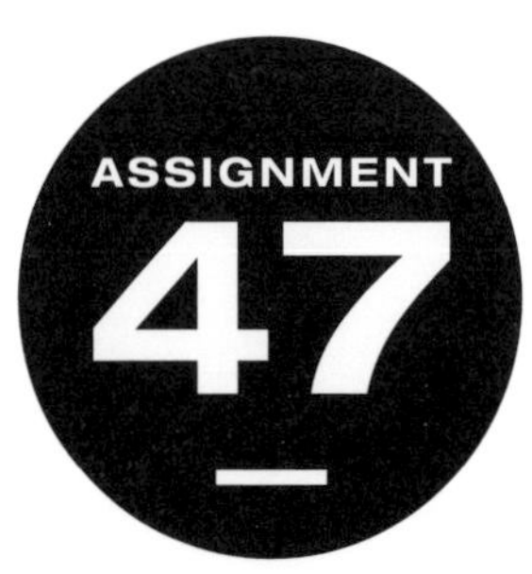

TECHNIQUE

- Find a subject with a strong personality—this will help form the essence of your image.

- Spend a little time with your subject before the shoot, ideally informally, to get a feel for their personality.

- If your subject is in the public eye, use desk-based research to find out as much as you can about them (including looking through any existing portraits). The more you know about them, the more you can chat to them. This natural, easy conversation will help achieve a relaxed portrait.

- Don't be overly deferential, even if your subject is well known. Speak to them as an equal and aim to have a relaxed conversation.

ASSIGNMENT JOURNAL

PRO TIP

If you haven't attempted this kind of portrait before, it can seem rather daunting—and the first one is always the most difficult. However, once you've shot a few of these, it will feel more natural.

▶ *This former British prime minister was on the campaign trail and was keen to exude a determined persona. A little research meant that there was a lot to talk about.*

BE YOURSELF

A big part of portrait photography is the ability to reveal the true character of the subject, letting their personality shine through. Once we start to cajole someone into adopting an alter ego for the sake of the camera, things can start to look forced.

But there's more to it than simply saying, "Be yourself." This assignment is all about getting to know your subject, putting them at ease, and developing a mutual understanding. Part of our role as photographers is to really connect with the person in front of the camera so that they will feel relaxed enough to reveal their true self to us. This rapport doesn't always come naturally to us but it's something that, over time and with practice, should become second nature.

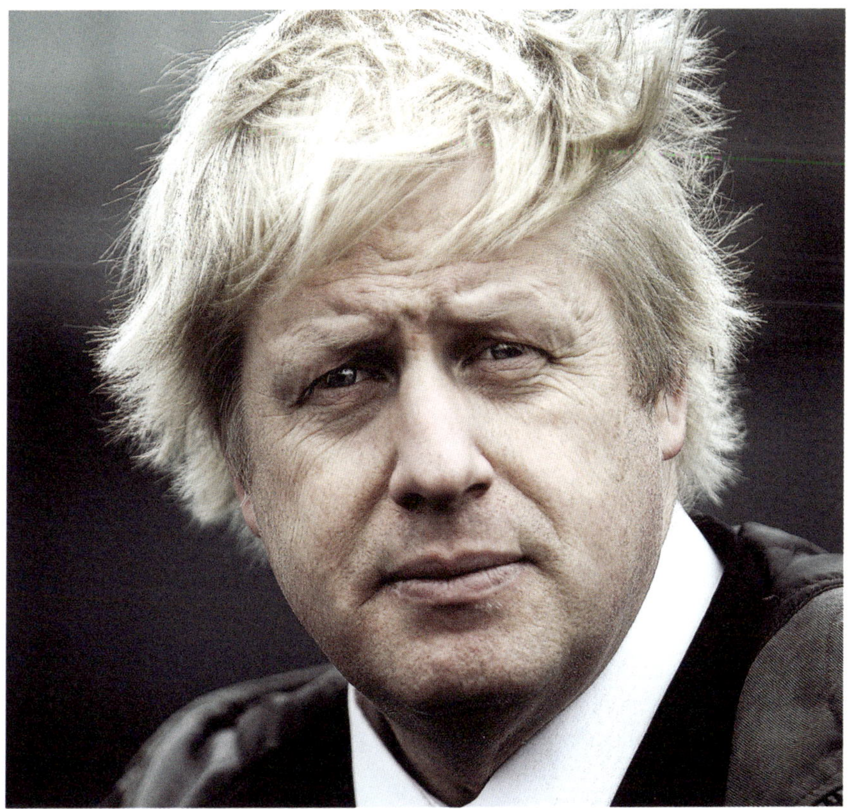

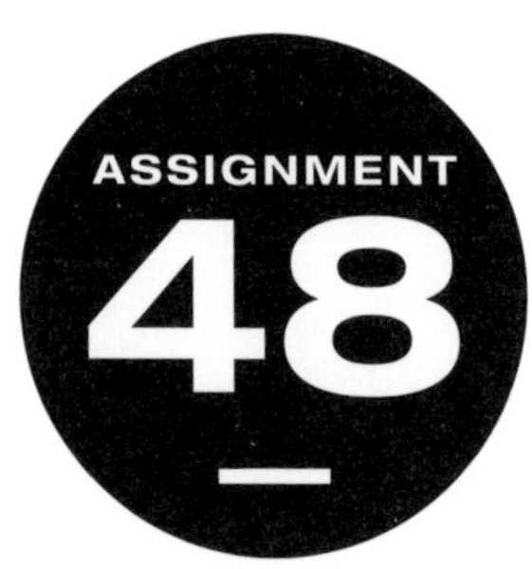

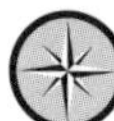

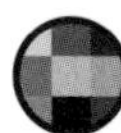

PRO TIP

Switch on any table or other occasional lamps, as they can look rather dull and uninteresting when they're unlit and can bring life to darker corners.

TECHNIQUE

- Shoot wide—a focal length between 28mm and 35mm should allow you to strike the right balance between portrait and interior.

- If you're relying on ambient light, shutter speeds will be slow so a tripod may be necessary. If you're short of space, a monopod should do the trick.

- Set up the lighting for the person first, then think about the room. Consider using a mixture of flash and ambient light and ensure the transitions between darker and lighter parts of the room are gradual and soft. You may need to subtly dodge and burn in post-production to achieve this.

- This is all about the details so make sure there are no stray coffee cups, newspapers, toys, etc. that could ruin the shot.

- If any surfaces are in direct light, make sure they're clean and free of dust.

HOUSE STYLE

Flick through a few glossy lifestyle magazines and you'll see plenty of portraits of people in their homes. These pictures are designed to show the living space as much as the people within it and need to be carefully lit and posed.

This assignment combines elements of both portrait and interiors photography and relies as much on the background as the subject to tell a story. Because you'll be dealing with different light sources (and therefore light temperatures) and varying areas of light and shade, it can be technically challenging from a lighting point of view, but it's a great exercise to get you thinking about light shapes, colors, and intensities.

Before the shoot, look through some interiors magazines to get a feel for what makes these images successful, try to work out how they were lit, and study different posing styles. Rip out relevant pages and create a mood board of ideas.

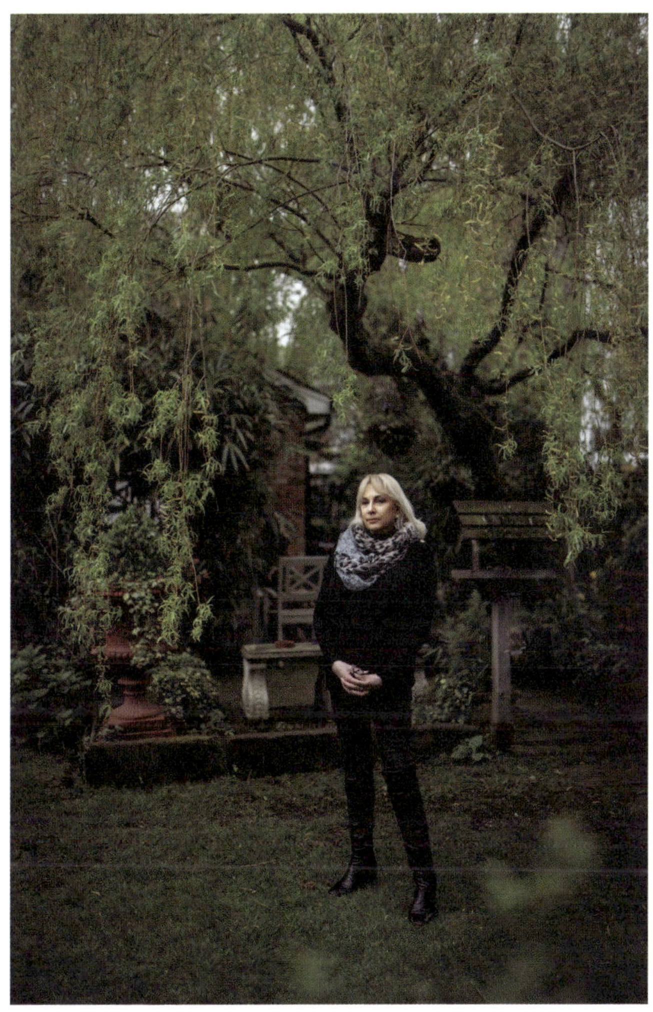

▲ *Have a thorough walk-through of the property before you start shooting and make a note of all the possible locations for your portraits. Don't forget to consider outside spaces.*

Key considerations include the size of the person in relation to their surroundings—you'll probably want to experiment with different ratios—and how your portrait is going to be lit. If you're using flash, several flash heads will probably be required to ensure even light coverage. If you're relying on natural light, be careful to avoid "hotspots" where the highlights will be blown out. Consider bouncing the light off pale walls or ceilings.

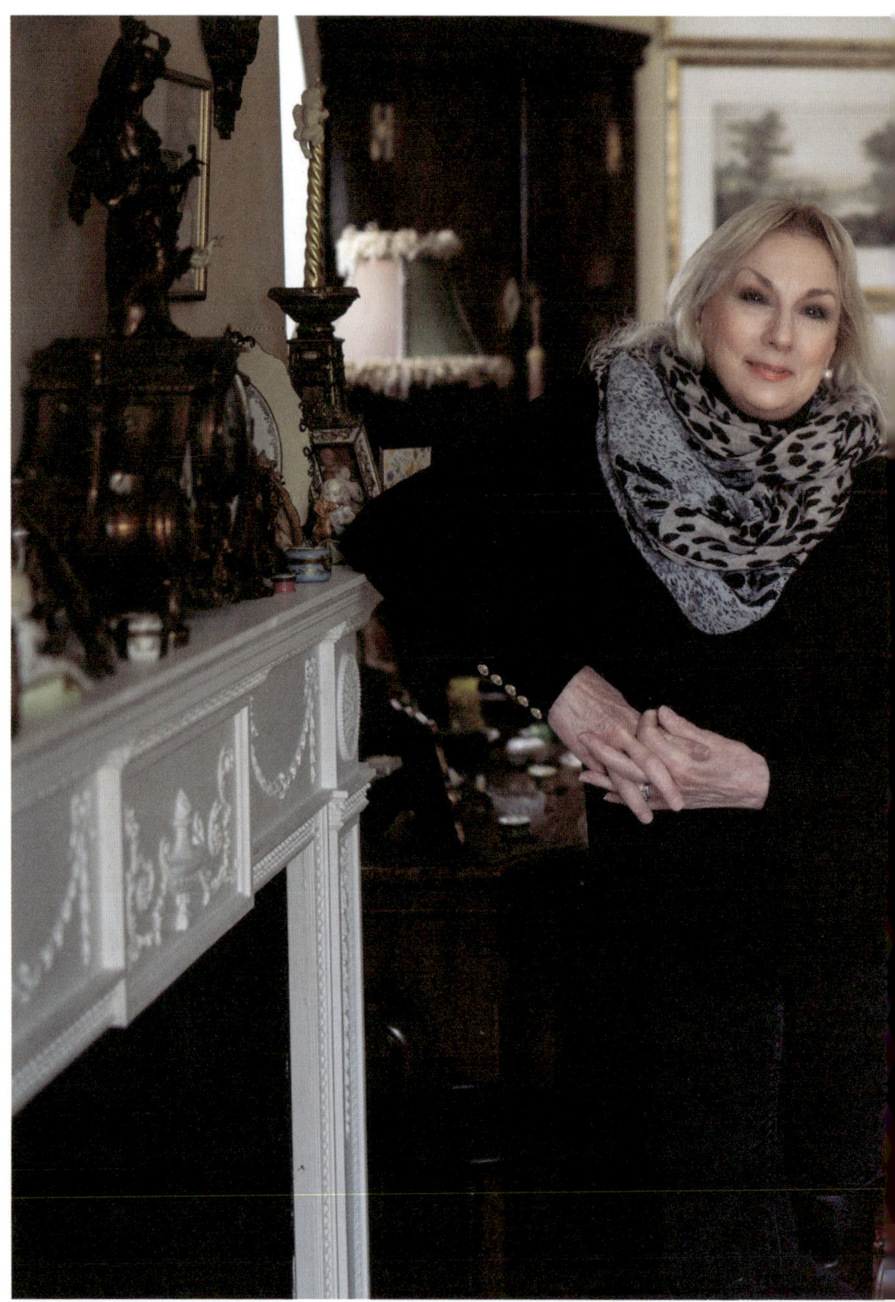

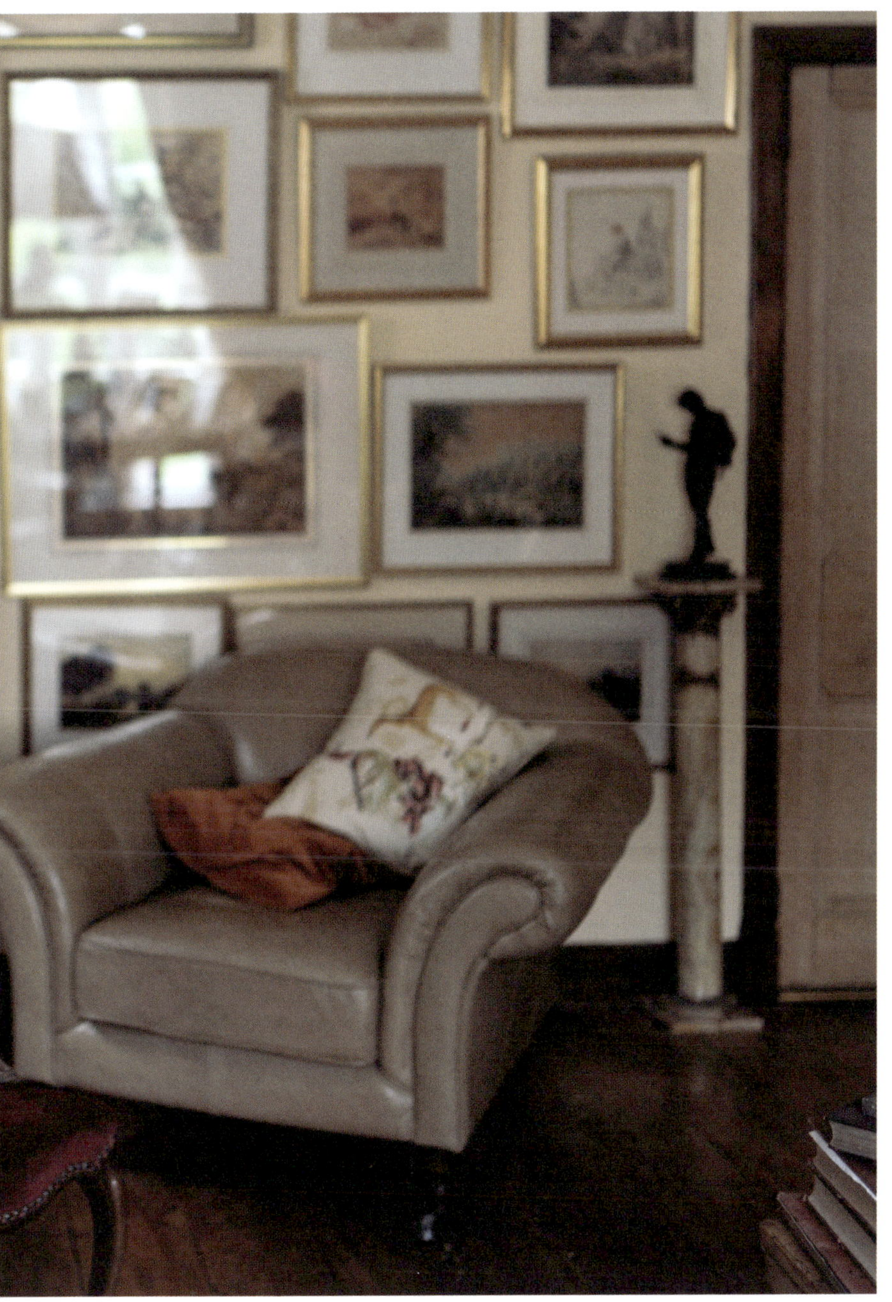

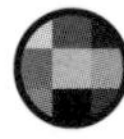

TECHNIQUE

- The sun is at its coolest mid-to-late morning, which is the safest time to shoot. Avoid looking directly at the sun.

- Focus on your subject's face and use spot metering to get an accurate exposure reading. Check the highlights and make sure the sky isn't completely blown out.

- Don't worry about underexposure in the shadows because you'll be surprised how much detail is recorded by the camera sensor in this part of the dynamic range. Using exposure compensation will help temper the strength of the bright sky.

- Compose your frame and then turn the camera away so the sun is just outside the field of view. Meter, recompose, and shoot.

- Consider using a reflector or fill-in flash to bounce light back onto the face.

- Use a lens hood and, ideally, a prime lens, and ensure your lens is completely clean.

- To help prevent overexposure on the face, try "hiding" the sun behind your subject.

PRO TIP

Try to include some translucent materials such as flowers or leaves in your frame—the backlighting will reward you with beautiful levels of detail and color, adding an extra layer of depth.

CONTRE-JOUR LIGHTING

Contre-jour (French for "against daylight") is a technique in which we point the camera directly toward the source of light to create a contrasty, backlit image. Sometimes we have no option but to shoot toward the light while other times we do it deliberately for creative effect. For this assignment, we're taking the deliberate approach and your light source will be the sun.

It's a challenging approach from an exposure point of view but the results can be dramatic. Be prepared to experiment, particularly with the placement of your subject in relation to the sun, which can dramatically change the look and feel of the image.

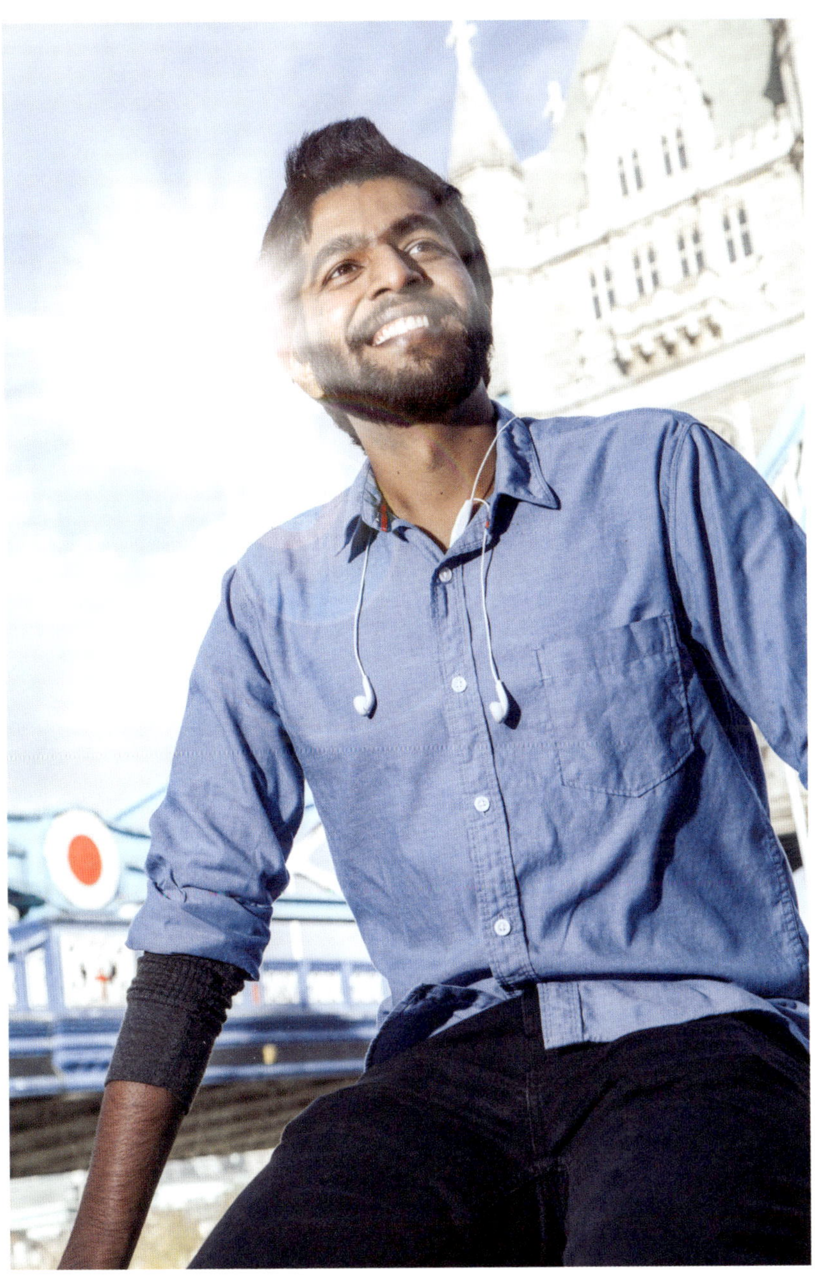

▲ *One of the by-products of contre-jour photography is lens flare. Instead of trying to eliminate it, why not embrace the effect and make it a feature of your portrait.*

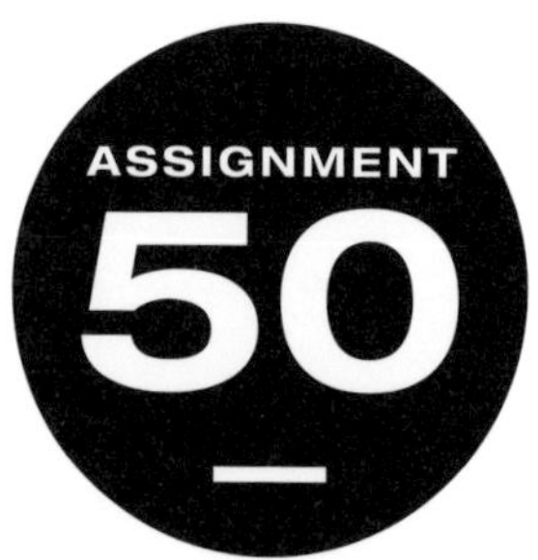

TECHNIQUE

- Focus on the subject rather than the prop—the latter should enhance the portrait, not take the viewer's attention away from it.

- Don't use too many props or different types of props, as this could be confusing and dilute the story or message.

- Choose a prop that's appropriate to the location you're shooting in. For example, if you're taking a portrait on a farm, you could use a tractor as the principal prop.

ASSIGNMENT JOURNAL

PRO TIP

Your role, as well as being the photographer, is stylist. It's your job to ensure the prop is relevant to the subject and to the "look" you're aiming to achieve, and that the prop's size, scale, content, and color all "work."

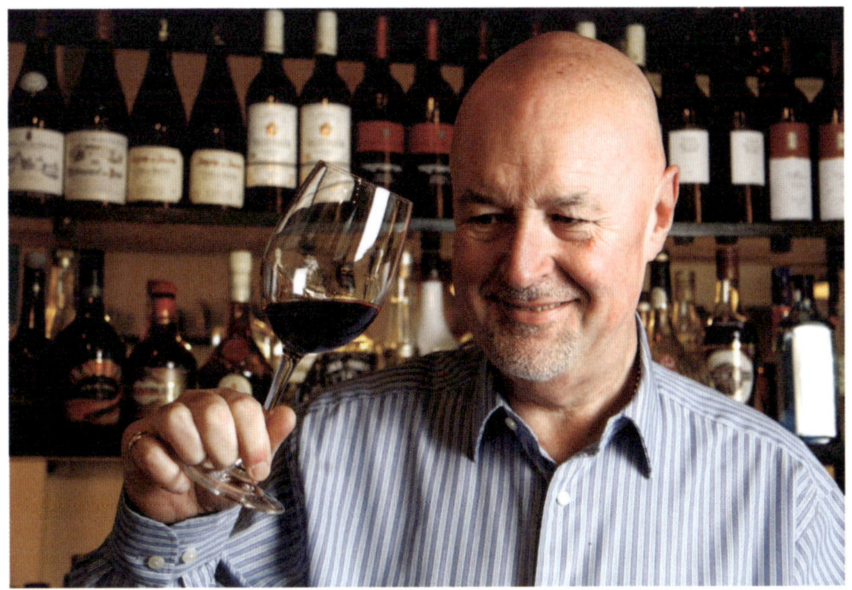

▲ *If you're using more than one prop (in this case, the wine bottles and glass behind the subject), ensure they work well together and look like they belong.*

USE A PROP

Using a prop in your portrait is a great way to tell your subject's story or reinforce a specific message. A prop could relate to the subject's lifestyle or interests (for example, a football trophy, a chess set, or sewing machine), or their work (a set of chef's knives or artisan's tools).

Even if your original intention is not to use a prop, it's worth suggesting to a reticent or nervous subject that they bring along a familiar prop to help them feel relaxed.

Your task is to shoot a portrait in which the prop is an integral part of the image, there as a creative choice, not an afterthought, as though the portrait wouldn't work without it. Work out in advance the story you want to tell and choose the prop(s) accordingly. They should complement but not overpower your subject, for example a florist with a small bunch of flowers or a butcher with a gleaming cleaver.

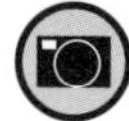

TECHNIQUE

- Shoot in close proximity using a 50mm lens or focal length, or from slightly further away using a longer lens or focal length such as 85mm or 135mm.

- Use a wide aperture to blur the background and make your subject "pop" but remember that focusing needs to be spot on.

- If your subject's head isn't square on to the camera, focus on the eye closest to the lens—with a wide aperture, it's unlikely you'll get both eyes in focus.

- Position your subject relative to the light source to eliminate any harsh shadows.

- Position your subject off-center using the rule of thirds to create a more balanced and interesting composition.

PRO TIP

Skin imperfections will be more evident close-up so you may need to do a little retouching. If your subject has shiny skin, a little powder can make a big difference, as can covering up any blemishes with make-up (though be careful not to overdo this). Most post-production apps have a "healing" brush for cleaning up skin and removing imperfections.

ZOOM IN FOR IMPACT

It was Robert Capa, the legendary photojournalist, who said, "If your pictures aren't good enough, you're not close enough." And it's a maxim we can sometimes use in portrait photography. A close-up portrait can reveal a lot about a person, filling the frame and allowing you to see right into their eyes. There's no doubt you can create a powerful and evocative portrait by getting close, but this assignment isn't about cropping in post-production—you need to get a true close-up at the point of capture.

This assignment is designed to encourage you to fill the frame for maximum impact. You'll discover the importance of detail (watch out for stray hairs, dandruff, etc.) and the subtle effects that can be achieved by the smallest changes to the lighting. It will test your ability to make fine adjustments to exposure settings, pose, and lighting.

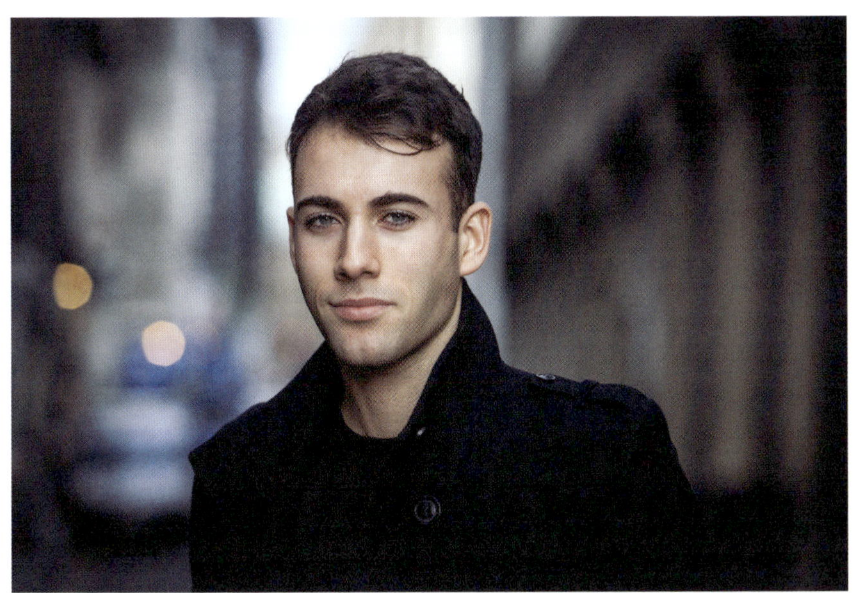

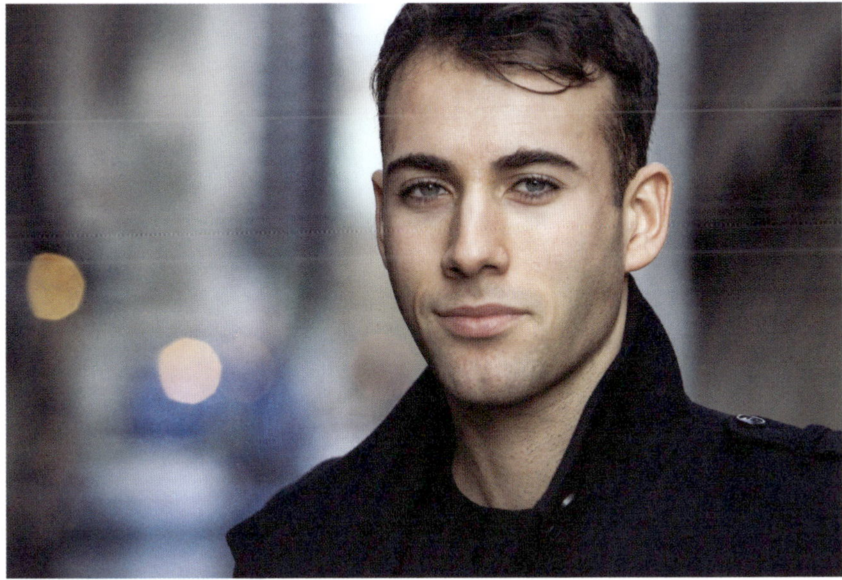

▲ *The zoomed-in portrait is more powerful, dynamic, and engaging than the wider shot. This is a great technique if you have a distracting background.*

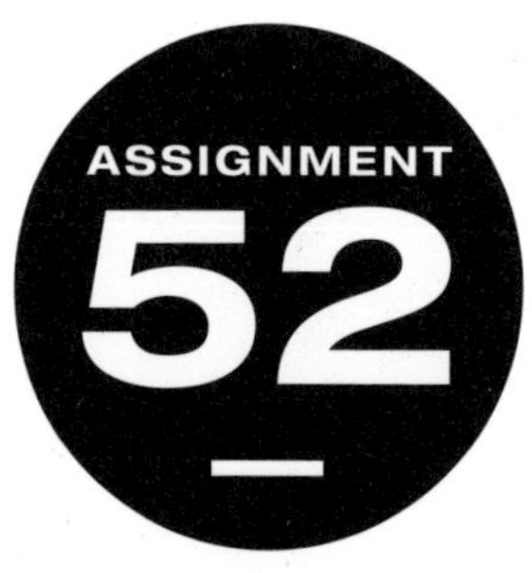

ASSIGNMENT

52

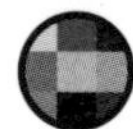

Continuous light such as an LED panel makes it easier to judge the effects of the light. If you're using a studio flash head, try using just the modeling light (most flash heads have a light bulb as well as the flash head, which is used to assess the light falling on the subject before the picture is taken).

ASSIGNMENT JOURNAL

TECHNIQUE

- Shoot in manual mode to maintain careful control of exposure.

- Position the light around 45° to the side of the subject and above their head.

- A fast shutter speed such as 1/125 sec. or 1/1250 sec. will help subdue the light not falling on your subject. Stay within your camera's maximum sync speed to avoid the shutter closing before the flash has been fully captured by the sensor, resulting in black bands across the frame.

- If your flash has a high-speed sync (HSS) mode, a fast shutter speed of around 1/2000 sec. should eliminate any stray light.

- To maintain a dark background, position your subject well away from it—around 6ft (2m) is ideal, as this avoids light from the flash hitting the background and lightening it.

- If you're using a light modifier such as a softbox or beauty dish, attaching a grid will help prevent the light spilling onto the background.

- Think about how the pose can help reinforce the feeling of "darkness." Asking your subject to look down is a good starting point.

▶ *Don't worry too much if the subject merges into the background—it's all part of the desired look.*

HIT THE LOW NOTES

We sometimes use low-key lighting to create portraits with mood, atmosphere, and drama. This style of lighting tends to be rich in contrast and shadows, with dark color tones and very few highlights and midtones.

This minimal low-key approach needs minimal kit—just one speedlight, flash head, or continuous light will suffice. Alternatively, you could use a focused beam of natural light, for example from the slat of a window blind.

This assignment will help you appreciate that portraiture isn't all about bright, happy images and that sometimes a more somber approach can help tell a story in a powerful way. Choose your subject carefully—this approach will work better for some people than for others.

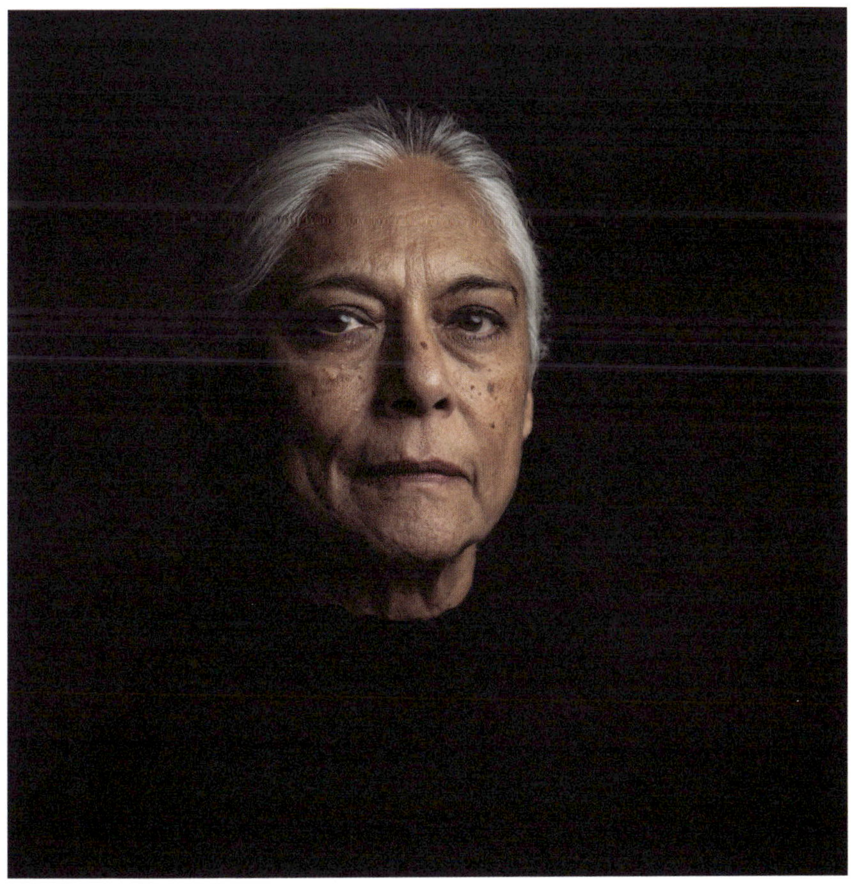

INDEX

A

First published 2023 by
Ammonite Press
an imprint of Guild of Master Craftsman Publications Ltd
Castle Place, 166 High Street, Lewes, East Sussex, BN7 1XU,
United Kingdom

ISBN 978-1-78145-479-4

Publisher: Jonathan Bailey
Production Director: Jim Bulley
Design Manager: Robin Shields
Designer: Rhiann Bull
Senior Project Editor: Tom Kitch
Editor: Ben Hawkins

Color reproduction by GMC Reprographics
Printed and bound in China

ACKNOWLEDGMENTS
To Johannah, Alex, and Maisie, who have patiently put up with my "writer's
temperament" during the writing of this book. Also, big "thank yous" to my
editor, Ben, for his insights and attention to detail, and to Fujifilm UK who kindly
provided me with materials and gave me the use of their Covent Garden
studio to shoot some of the images for this book. Most of all, I would like
to thank all the people who have been willing (and not so willing!)
models for me—I couldn't have done this without you.

How was the book?
Please post your
feedback and photos:
#52AssignmentsPortrait

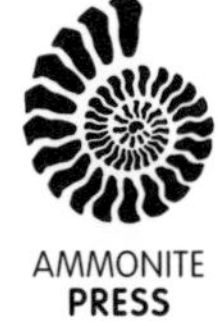

AMMONITE
PRESS

ammonitepress.com

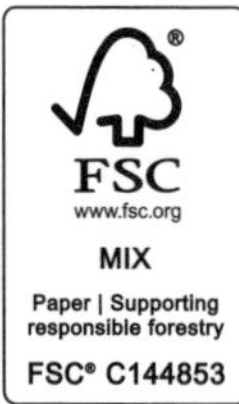